D0787888

YOUR POWER TO BE

J. SIG PAULSON

Your Power To Be

DOUBLEDAY & COMPANY, INC.
GARDEN CITY, NEW YORK

The author is grateful to the following publishers for permission to use copyrighted material:

Daily Word for the poems "Love's Awakening" and "I Love People" by J. Sig Paulson. Grosset & Dunlap, Inc., Publisher, for material from *As a Man Thinketh* by James Allen. Unity Books for material from *The Symphony of Life* by Donald Hatch Andrews.

Special thanks are due to Dr. Donald Hatch Andrews for his kind authorization to use portions of his personal letter to the author.

*This book is gratefully dedicated
to two adventurous and inspiring
teammates in the game of life—
my sons, Terry and Jon.*

GRATITUDE

Thank you,
Marie Lee Hess,
for your faith,
your enthusiasm and your persistence.

FOREWORD

This book is written for the spiritually adventurous—those who are ready to walk the largely uncharted paths of their own souls. It is not particularly a religious book; some may even feel that it is nonreligious or even irreligious. To me, the ideas shared in this book are based on the teaching of the Bible—not just an outer Bible, but more importantly the inner Bible which is the law or potential written in the inner being of man.

I am convinced that we are entering the time long-foretold when God, the Spirit of Truth within, will be the teacher of every man. We are witnessing the breaking up and passing away of the former power structures of the world. Religious institutions, social, economic and governmental systems, myths, superstitions, ignorance and limitation that have held sway over man for centuries are making way for the man of light, the man of Spirit, created in the image of his Maker. This is a time of turmoil and upheaval. The old order is passing away and the shape of the new comes only in flashes of insight and inspiration. But the end is at hand. Man is surrendering to his own potential as the offspring of the Almighty.

It is my earnest desire that this book will encourage you in your travel along the path that you must walk alone, under the guidance of your own Soul. Rejoice in knowing that there are many who consciously walk a similar, yet uniquely different, way. Be glad that you are blazing a trail, moving along a path that all humanity must someday join in following—the path of individual self-realization.

Dare to lift your vision—of God—of yourself—of your neighbor. Move confidently into the life you are designed to live.

CONTENTS

with Approval Your Body and You The Second
Commandment No Minor Skirmish To Start the
Flow of Approval Don't Withhold Approval Love
Through Approval.

YOUR POWER TO BE

1

THE RELIGIOUS EXPLOSION

The human scene is rocked by explosions that mark the breaking up of an old world of belief and experience. Knowledge explosions, population explosions, racial explosions, are shattering the foundations of a social structure that had been building for centuries. An old world is slipping into the wastebasket of eternity, and the shape of the new world being brought forth on the stage of human experience is only dimly perceived. Everything that man has believed is being questioned in the light of the scientific breakthrough. Cherished beliefs are being discarded, and venerable institutions are coming apart at the seams as the healthy breeze of inquiry blows through them. While occasional voices are raised in an attempt to preserve the old order, they usually speak with more volume than authority, and the status quo and the status past are no longer powerful enough to stem the tide of change.

Explosive charges are going off in the area of religion, too. After centuries of growing affluence and waning influence, institutionalized religion is being boldly challenged, not so much by sinful men to whom it had become adjusted, but by thinking men who probe into its foundations, question its doctrines and usefulness, and even theorize that its God is dead! The comfortable pulpit is no longer so comfortable, and the upholstered pew is proving to be hard sitting for those who venture into the lofty cathedrals of modern religion in search of the bread of life. For hundreds of years, much of the professional clergy has been sitting on its collective bottom, spiritually speaking, rising to its feet once or twice a week to preach prosaic sermons in language often incomprehensible to anyone but its own members. Members of congregations, nominally the target for the religious rhetoric, for the most part gave up trying to follow the complicated doctrines and obscure language and settled for an enforced hour of dutiful inattention, assuming that they had fulfilled their religious obligations and made at least a down payment on a ticket for some future paradise in the sky. To enliven the religious scene, the professionals often engaged in arguments with each other on subjects ranging from the number of angels who could dance on the head of a pin, to weightier matters like the virgin birth, the crucifixion of Jesus Christ, the grace of God, and even the nature of the hell to which sinners and nonconformists would be consigned for eternity.

RELIGION AND SCIENCE

Assuming that they already had all the truth that was available, many religious leaders tightly closed their minds, drew their doctrines neatly about them, and settled stiffly down behind the barriers of denominational bias and exclusivitis. From these stout and virtually unassailable positions, they religiously resisted new ideas and the resurgence of old truths until they became bothersome; then they embraced many of the revelations and buried them in the trappings and rituals of organized religion. Fortunately, when religion sat down on the job of seeking, science, which is the research department of truth, took up the task of probing into the nature of the universe, and its discoveries are now forcing leaders of religion to take another look at the gods it has been worshiping.

As a matter of fact, in many ways a new religion is emerging, and its high priests are the leaders and researchers of the scientific world. Open minds in both the religious and scientific fields are observing the unity of these two areas of human endeavor, and hopefully the stage is being set for a combined effort to wipe out the ignorance that has held man in bondage. Rare individuals like

Pierre Teilhard de Chardin seem much at home in both fields, and no doubt others will catch and expand his vision, tentatively at first, then with increasing power and authority.

In earlier times, religion and science were on the same team, and they will have to be again if our scientific discoveries are to be used for the benefit of humanity and not its destruction. If religion is to be an effective member of the team and bring forth guidelines that will help to keep humanity intact, it will have to rise above its role of institutionalized social service, building schools, churches, and hospitals, important though these are. It will have to rise above its role of frustrated bookkeeper of men's sins and morals. It will have to rise above its role of pointer to the blessings of the paradise in the great beyond. It will have to become what it is designed to be—a channel for the truth that sets men free here and now from the bondage, the ignorance, the frustrations, the bitterness, the separateness of daily living.

THE TRAGIC MISCONCEPTIONS

To be a channel for the truth, of course, organized religion operating under the name of Christianity will find it necessary to eliminate the superstitions, half-truths and non-truths that have plagued it for hundreds of years. Even an enforced examination of its own underpinnings will be an eye- and mind-opener. The misconceptions of God, the Creator, man and the universe will be readily discerned if not easily accepted, and a new, vital religion will be the result. I recall that as a youngster on the Montana plains I used to hear the cowboys sing a mournful little ditty about the pains of living twenty years with the "wrong" woman. Living twenty years (or twenty centuries!) with the "wrong" religion is even tougher, but that has been the experience of much of humanity!

The organized Christian religion has built an outer structure based on a misconception of both the nature of man and the church. Much of the authority for this outer structure comes from a superficial interpretation of the scripture found in Matthew 16:13–20:

> Now when Jesus came into the district of Caesarea Philippi, he asked his disciples, "Who do men say that the Son of man is?" And they said, "Some say John the Baptist, others say Elijah, and others Jeremiah or

one of the prophets." He said to them, "But who do you say that I am?"
Simon Peter replied, "You are the Christ, the Son of the living God."
And Jesus answered him, "Blessed are you, Simon Bar-Jona! For flesh
and blood has not revealed this to you, but my Father who is in heaven.
And I tell you, you are Peter, and on this rock I will build my church,
and the powers of death shall not prevail against it. I will give you
the keys of the kingdom of heaven, and whatever you bind on earth
shall be bound in heaven, and whatever you loose on earth shall be
loosed in heaven." Then he strictly charged the disciples to tell no one
that he was the Christ.

OUTER CHURCH ORGANIZATION

Organizers of religion have seized on this scripture as the authority for an outer church organization, governed by a select hier-
archy of priests, ministers, and other religious figures, supposedly
operating with varying degrees of infallibility, based on lines reportedly established by a man called Peter. Strong leaders of this
outer church organization have assumed that heaven is a special
piece of real estate somewhere in distant space and time, where
bliss reigns supreme and to which they held secure title. They
have preached that God is an angry despot who demanded the
bloody death of His only Son, Jesus, before opening the gates of
Heaven through the narrow gates of denominational bias the
angry preachers served. Failing to gain enough converts by this
distorted vision, they often sought to herd humanity into heaven
by trying to scare the "hell" out of it—and since "sinners" were
going to wind up in hell anyway, they have not hesitated to
institute inquisitions, holy wars and witch drownings to usher the
poor wretches off the earth as quickly and painfully as possible.

There is no point in documenting too much of the dark religious
past—remnants still operate in human thought and feeling—after
all, religious leaders were not all to blame . . . laymen were just
about as ignorant as their priests and teachers. Truly the "blind
were leading the blind" down the path of destruction, war and
separation right here on earth.

THE "NON-CHURCHY" MAN

Surely it is beginning to dawn in the enlightened minds of both
professional clergy and ordinary human beings that Jesus was about

the most "non-churchy" man who ever walked the earth. He was in almost constant conflict with the operators of the religious combine of His day, and it is doubtful that the vested interests of this age would be any more comfortable with His nontraditional approach to religion than were the religious authorities of 2000 years ago.

Jesus tried to take religion out of the hands of the professional religionists, out of the temples and synagogues, and to put it where it has always belonged—in the mind and heart of each individual. His special project has been long delayed because of the slowness of both clergy and laymen to accept the explosive truth He taught and demonstrated, but the time foretold has arrived, and the spirit of Truth is being stirred in minds and hearts all around the world.

You are probably one in whom this spirit is stirring, or you wouldn't be reading this book—so I think you will enjoy reading this scripture again in a slightly different form. I have inserted in brackets silent ideas which the teaching of Jesus indicate should be there.

> Now when Jesus came into the district of Caesarea Philippi, he asked his disciples, "Who do men say that the Son of man is?" And they said, "Some say John the Baptist, others say Elijah, and others Jeremiah or one of the prophets." He said to them, "But who do you say that I am?" Simon Peter replied, "You are the Christ, the Son of the living God." And Jesus answered him, "Blessed are you, Simon Bar-Jona! For flesh and blood has not revealed this to you, but my Father who is in heaven. And I tell you, you are [the Christ, the Son of the living God] Peter, and on this rock [the Christ within] I will build my church, and the powers of death shall not prevail against it. I will give [the Spirit of Truth within] you the keys of the kingdom of heaven, and whatever you bind on earth shall be bound in heaven, and whatever you loose on earth shall be loosed in heaven." Then he strictly charged the disciples to tell no one that he was the Christ.

THE INNER CHURCH

It seems quite obvious that to Jesus the church was not an outer religious organization or institution—rather it was an inner institution based on the divine constitution of man. The Church of Christ is to be built on sounder ground than any outer organization, even one supposedly based on the inspiration of a dedicated man. It is to be built on solid rock—the Spirit of God in man—and the powers of death, ignorance and strife will not prevail against it. In spite of all opposition, it is now coming to light, and the true and explosive teaching of Jesus Christ will soon be taught to all mankind.

If the professional church can shake its lethargy, inertia, tradition and complacency it can be an agent for this explosion in religion—if not, it will be taught elsewhere and the fine church buildings in the United States will be as empty as are the cathedrals in many other sections of the world. The time is late, the pressure is great—so let's examine the teaching of Jesus Christ.

THE KINGDOM OF GOD

First, let's start with God. Jesus said that God is Spirit, and that those who worship God rightly must do so in spirit and in truth—not on some holy mountain or in some cathedral or church. (See John 4:19–25)

Then, what about the kingdom of God, or heaven? First, its location—He said that it would not come through observation, because the kingdom of God is within you. (See Luke 17:20–21)

And its nature? Jesus said it is like a grain of mustard seed which when sown in the ground becomes a great tree; or like a sower who goes out to sow; or like a man who sowed good seed in his field and an enemy came and sowed bad seed and complications followed; or like a woman putting leaven in three measures of meal until all was leavened; or like a treasure hidden in a field found by a farmer who sells all to get it; or a merchant who sells all to obtain a fine pearl. (See Matthew 13:1–51)

And who holds the key to the mysteries of this inner kingdom? The Spirit of Truth that Jesus said He would send to lead you into all truth. (See John 16:7–15) Jesus said that finding this inner kingdom of spirit and truth was a job we cannot pass on to someone else, no matter how well he may seem qualified by human standards. We must seek and find it for ourself, and doing this should be our number one project. (See Luke 12:29–32)

We have entered the age of individual spiritual unfoldment. The finger of eternity is on you and me. We cannot evade responsibility, or pin blame on others. We have the opportunity to rise out of the ignorance, fear and superstition of the past. You and I can shake the inertia of both past and present and begin to follow Jesus Christ into the kingdom of God within.

Here are some mind stretchers to consider: "Heaven is not a physical paradise. It is the kingdom of God, Spirit, Creative Energy within me. My leader in my search for the kingdom is the Spirit of Truth within. It is leading me into all the truth. My church is the temple of the living God that I am—and that you are!"

Charles Fillmore, co-founder of the Unity movement, pointed out that there is a church or worship service going on in each individual all of the time, but most are too occupied with outer things to know it.

2

THE POWER TO BE

It is much easier to deify a man and make him a "savior" than it is to follow his example, to plug into the power he demonstrates and give it self-expression. There are, and have been, many who profess to "believe in" Jesus Christ, who call Him their savior, and who expect to ride into heaven (paradise) on his coattails because of the sacrifice he made to appease an angry god who was about to scrap mankind and toss it on the junk heap of eternal damnation. If there ever was such a god to appease, that god is dead and Jesus Christ was one of the first to pull the trigger that killed him! Of course, the only god that could die is one that never really lived, except in the ignorant, frightened minds of men. If god is dead, it is in the sense that a "flat" earth is dead; that the concept of a solid, material universe is dead or dying; that the concept of religious and racial "superiority" is dead or dying, or that all the narrow, restricted beliefs that have held mankind in bondage are gradually dissolving and dying out as the light of truth goes on in human consciousness.

YOUR TRUE ESTATE

Jesus pulled the trigger that shot the anthropomorphic god out of the sky when He revealed that God is Spirit or universal creative energy and that the kingdom or dwelling place of that spiritual energy is in man; and that man, when he seeks out and expresses that inner power, is destined to be the agency through which the world of the future is to be governed. It is finally dawning on many who are moving from *believing in* Jesus Christ to *believing* Him, that the "God power" that is to rule any paradise of the future is now buried in man, awaiting his acceptance and expression of it.

The Bible tells us that all who received "the true light" were given the power to become children of God, and that they were no longer bound by the limitations of flesh and blood, or the will of man, but became new creatures, being born of God.

Heaven is the paradise that will be brought into expression when man exercises the power to be what he is created to be—and hell is the world of limitation, sickness, war and misery in which he struggles until he becomes fully conscious of his true estate.

THE DIVINE POTENTIAL

Scientific research indicates that the whole outer universe is energy in one form or another, and that this energy is completely responsive to direction that can maintain or intensify the present state of "hell on earth," or bring forth a paradise for all, if properly and lovingly redirected. Atomic energy, for example, can be used to wipe out civilization or to make the "desert blossom like the rose." It should be pretty obvious that there is no outer god who is about to yell, "Whoa, boys. You've gone far enough; I'm coming down to earth to take over and establish peace among men and nations."

The God who is to save mankind, if it is to be saved, is the divine potential within humanity itself, the celestial spark within each individual, or as St. Paul describes it: "Christ in you, your hope of glory," or as Jesus described it: "The Spirit of Truth" that is to lead man into all truth.

There isn't much doubt any longer that this universe is designed as a dwelling place for a race of gods. The energies that are being brought to light in the physical, mental and emotional departments of being are just too great and powerful to be handled adequately by the ignorant, frightened, belligerent, warlike creature that man has been. The next great step in human evolution is at hand, and all mankind is soon to see what formerly only the enlightened could perceive: Each individual is the child (off-spring) of God (to put it in religious terms)—or the self-expression of the universal creative energy, to say it in another way. And to each individual is given the responsibility and opportunity to seek, find and express the kingdom of creative energy within his own being.

No person is exempt from this responsibility or opportunity and no person can get away with assigning it to church, state, society or other "savior." There is no, as we say, "passing the buck" or evading our share of what needs to be done in this spiritual age.

YOUR ROLE IN THE NEW AGE

If you are intelligent, open-minded and confident enough to be reading this book without too much inner conflict, you are already well on the way to your role in the new age, and you will continue to read with growing insight and enthusiasm. You are ready for an adventure in living that will move you rapidly out of old ruts of thought, feeling and experience. The ideas and words shared with you are not intended as rigid outlines for you to follow—you are already spiritually independent enough to reject any attempt to pressure you into any course of action—they are offered to encourage you to trust your own inner integrity and inspiration and to follow the guidance of the spirit of Truth in you.

If, on the other hand, this book seems to contradict your basic beliefs, or is too much to swallow, it is better that you set it aside for the time being or give it to a friend who is no longer satisfied with conventional religious approaches to life. I say in all sincerity that if you read this book, either in agreement or argument, and either apply or fight the courses of action suggested, you will be a changed person, whether you want to be or not.

This is easy for me to predict, because I have seen the ideas I am writing about work the miracle of change in countless lives. The ideas are not new—they have been buried in one form or another in all the great religions of mankind—they are part of the truth that is the common, or should I say, the extraordinary, possession of all mankind, regardless of religious profession. So, if you are not too comfortable or set in your present state, prepare yourself for the experience of a complete change in your thinking, feeling, actions and personality.

THE GREAT STEP

A woman who had been working with a number of these ideas told me she had a pleasant and unexpected experience when she met a friend she had not seen for several years. This friend said: "My, you've changed. You used to be a regular worry-wart. You were always half sick, afraid of what people thought about you, ready to join our circle of gossip. Now you seem so relaxed and radiant. What happened?" The woman who shared this experience with me laughed and said: "You know, I must have changed tremendously. I couldn't even remember myself as the person my friend described."

It is a wonderful adventure to receive the "true light" and to begin to exercise the "power to be" children of God—the self-expression of the creative Spirit that produced us.

The decision to take this great step is up to us. If we wait for some religious authority, a priest, minister, or denominational representative to stick a thermometer into us and decide that we are spiritually mature enough before we make the plunge, we will never get started. We are moving into a new era of human experience and unfoldment. The yardsticks of the past are out—your experience, your insight, your progress, are just as valid and just as important as anyone else's. No other person can establish a tight, little format for you to follow—all he can do is to share experiences, insights and revelations that he has gained from traveling on his own path of unfoldment. Conventional obstacles from both your outer world and your inner world of past belief and experience may be hurled at you, but if you are wise, you will neither fight nor accept them—rather you will let yourself grow beyond them, and they will dissolve without too much effort on your part.

THE CREATIVE AND THE CREATED

The greatest power in the universe is the power to be! It expresses itself in every created thing. A drop of water, a blade of grass, a planet, a star, a dog, a cat, a bird, are all expressions of the power to be. It is in man that the power to be finds its greatest expression and its greatest potential. It is in man that the Godhead or Power to Be is to find individual expression, and this expression is to come about through the co-operation of the creator and the created. Man is an instrument capable of infinite expansion as he awakens to his true identity and accepts his place in the divine scheme of things. In man, the creative Power to Be has produced a creature equipped to refine the evolutionary process, to accelerate its progress, and to use its energies consciously. Man can, and inevitably must, become conscious of his true nature as the self-expression of the universal Power to Be. Man, of all creatures, can say: "I am the power to be . . ." and then "write his own ticket" or choose the patterns through which the world of today and tomorrow will come. He can continue to rely on the patterns of his "earthy" past, his animal instincts, his fears, his superstitions, his limited concepts of himself and his world—or he can move, as St. Paul points out, to the patterns of "heavenly" man and give life to a new design, a new creature of light, love, joy and peace, in whom there is no darkness of ignorance, disease or death at all.

THE PLAN OF GOD

Jesus calls this process being born again. Jesus Christ was the "first fruits" of those (all humanity) who have been asleep to the inner potential, and we are to follow Him, not into some plush outer paradise, or piece of heavenly real estate—but in seeking and finding and expressing the inner kingdom of Spirit that brings forth a race of new creatures on the earth. The "heaven" toward which we are headed is the expression of the divine potential in man. Apparently, the only way to finish man was to put him into an unfinished universe whose problems are so great that humanity can solve them only by calling on the hidden, or at least unsuspected, God power within. This new and greater expression of the power to be is the business of everyone, not just a group of religious or scientific specialists. Every human being is a unit of expression, and the power to be is individualized, expressed and experienced in and by every person. This means that you and I are a living, vital part of the new world that is being born in the consciousness of mankind.

The true religion of today is the process by which each individual accepts and fulfills his role in the cosmic design of the universe; the plan of God, it might be called in the words of religious theology.

YOUR "I AM" POWER

It has been helpful to me to realize that I individualize the divine power to be every time I think, feel, speak or act as a person; that is, every time I exercise my "I AM" power, I individualize the Power to Be in my world. I give it a center and instrument of operation. In this connection, too, it is well to remember that the Old Testament teaches that the name (nature) of God from generation to generation forever is I AM. Even in my admittedly limited state of consciousness, I exercise the Power to Be over a tremendous range, as does every other man.

For example, and I feel you will easily join me in this, I can see that: I am the power to be peaceful or warlike; harmonious or irritated; happy or unhappy; generous or stingy; constructive or destructive in thought, feeling and action. These constitute obviously a fairly limited range of choices, representing mostly a pendulum of opposites that we exercise many times each day.

CHILDREN OF GOD

Jesus taught, however, if we are to accept the Bible as authority, that each individual's power to be is virtually unlimited because of his relationship to the Creator. Jesus called the Creator Father—and He not only claimed the divine fatherhood for Himself, He shared it with His listeners. He told them not to call any man on earth father because they had but one father, God. Then He also taught that we should pray to "Our Father, Who art in Heaven." If our father is God, then we must be children of the "Most High." Strange that most of the world of professing Christians could parrot this "Lord's Prayer" in countless churches throughout the centuries without having the light of truth break through in every mind!

I have talked with clergymen who admitted that in years of study they had never been exposed to the truth that every man is a child of God and that the divine kingdom is within the individual. Several years ago an outstanding priest told me that his whole life was transformed when he received a little magazine of daily devotions called *Daily Word*, and he read a lesson on the kingdom of God within man. He said his whole approach to working with people changed when he realized that they were not simply "sinners," but children of God, ignorant of their true identity. In one day, he told me, his whole ministry of service was lifted to a new level of understanding and appreciation. The miracle in his own being was repeated many times in the lives of those he served when they learned that God was not an angry despot in the sky, but rather the potential love, life and joy they were created to express.

HOW FAR DO YOU WANT TO GO?

Far from being angry with His ignorant children, Jesus revealed that God, Our Heavenly Father, is eager to give us the kingdom of good. It is our Father's "good pleasure" to give us the kingdom— and it will be our "good pleasure" to accept that kingdom and give it radiant expression in our world, once we come into an understanding of its nature and availability.

Jesus was a demonstrator of the kingdom of God (good) and those who accepted Him and His demonstration were given the power to be children of the same Father, and thus to be "saved" from their old states of ignorance, superstition and fear. The nature of the kingdom is described, according to the words of Jesus, in simple terms like light, life, love, forgiveness and joy—to name just a few of them.

Some of our latest scientific discoveries into the nature of the universe and of man give new insight into the simplicity and power of the teaching of Jesus, and it is the purpose of this book to encourage you who read it to start your own scientific research program into the nature of the kingdom of God within you. It is in large measure a "do-it-yourself" project. You are a unique, unlimited expression of the universal power to be, and only you can decide how far you wish to go. All anyone else can do is echo the revelation of Jesus: "The Kingdom of God is within you," and urge you to seek, find and express it, starting with your present understanding, faith and initiative. No other person, even Jesus, can do the job for us.

HIT THE WATER AND START SWIMMING

I am reminded of an experience I had when I was studying for the ministry. I had the opportunity of speaking to a large group of inmates in a penitentiary. In trying to make the point of the importance of personal involvement, I said: "If I wanted to learn to swim, I could approach the project in several ways. I could read a good book on the subject; I could talk to an expert swimmer; I could watch good swimmers—and in the process, perhaps I could write a best-selling book on swimming. But, if I really wanted to learn to swim, what would I have to do?" I paused for just a few moments before I delivered the final punch line—but I didn't have to—one of the listeners, a big, handsome fellow with twinkling eyes and acres of diamonds in his smile, shouted it for me: "Hit the water, brother, and start swimming."

It is time for us all to "hit the water and start swimming" in the kingdom of God, and as you continue to read I trust that you will find encouragement and inspiration from the ideas and courses of action shared. I think you will find it a happy and adventurous experience to let go of old concepts and ways of living —and that something pretty wonderful will take place in your world as the result. The shift in identity from varying degrees of "worthless sinner" to a son or daughter of God identity has to work miracles in all that concerns you. You are "on your own" in a wonderful sense, but that "own" is the infinite power to be within you, and you are in an interesting and adventurous company who share your experiences, thrills and even your ups and downs. Come on in, the water's fine.

3

WHAT DO YOU THINK?

Anyone who begins for the first time to worship in the church of his own being (the Church of Christ) is up against some formidable adversaries. Not only are most religious tradition, dogma and practice against such worship—he finds that his own thinking is so conditioned to outer forms that he hardly knows where to start. He is so accustomed to having his thinking made up by churches, institutions, political organizations, groups and other individuals that it is difficult to believe that within his own being there is a dependable power that is much more reliable. He is so firmly tied to the limitations of flesh-and-blood existence that to think he is a god, or even a distant relative of one, seems beyond his reach. He may ask with the Psalmist: "What is man that thou art mindful of him, and the Son of man, that thou visitest him?"

MASTERS OF THE WORLD?

And yet all of us have within the instincts and urges of godhood. We feel that we should be the master of our world. We are constantly working to overcome its problems, its diseases, its unhappinesses, its lacks, its bondage, its challenge. Through our scientific and technological breakthroughs, we are constantly exercising more effective control over our outer world, and learning more about its inner make-up. We are discovering that the tiniest particles of matter have much more energy in them than we could have dreamed just a few short years ago. And this type of discovery makes us stop and think a bit about man himself.

If, as one scientist points out, there is enough atomic energy in the atoms of the tip of a man's finger to supply the power needs of a great city for days, if it could be released, then what about man himself? his mind? his soul? his spirit? Who is this creature who probes into the universe, unlocks its secrets, unhooks the elements of the atom, rearranges the face of the earth and plans to fly to the unthinkable depths of space? Is it possible that deep within the mystery of his being there are undiscovered secrets, unfathomed energies, unsuspected potentials? Is it not likely that man has known as little of his own nature as he has known of the nature of the world in which he has been living? Can it be that man has been a sleeping god, ignorant of his own identity, just now beginning to awaken to his own role in the future development of the universe? Is it true that man is made just a mite lower than the angels—that he is the creature who is to have dominion over all creation when he discovers the reality of his own being and rightly utilizes the energies available for self-expression through him? Are descriptions of man as the image of God, the light of the world, a life-giving spirit just figments of a fertile imagination—or are they true? Does the universal power to be (God) individualize and surrender Its infinite energies to man in order to carry forth the great plan of evolutionary progression?

What do you think?

YOUR PRIVATE SANCTUARY

Here is a good place to start to worship in the Church of Christ, the sanctuary of your own being.

What do you think?

The first answer to this question may be a flood of ready-made answers inherited from your religious tradition, education and other forms of memory. But keep on asking the question until you get the feeling that the answer comes from a deeper source, a more intimate source than tradition, education or memory. Ultimately, you will become acquainted with, and learn to trust, the spirit (or feeling) of Truth within you, even if the answers that come through shake up your traditional religious beliefs and training.

Now, if you choose, your inner worship service can take a new turn, and you can begin to reidentify yourself. Following is a suggested pattern, but you might want to use different words. After all, this is your worship service, and you are running it:

I AM (individualize) the power to be _____.

Then fill in the blank with your own answers. There are some excellent ones from the Bible. For example, I AM the power to be the image of God. I AM the power to be the light of the world. I AM the power to be a life-giving spirit. Let your mind and heart expand on what you are doing. You are on your own. There is no long-nosed, bony-fingered, menacing figure looking down on you, to criticize or condemn. You are alone in the church of your choice, the temple of mind, heart and body that you are. Dare to do some experimenting. Try a few new images of yourself on for size. You can never come up with anything more wonderful than you really are!! Enjoy getting the feel of a new you.

THE TWELVE POWERS

In the chapters that follow we are going to deal with what has come to be known as the twelve powers of man. They are referred to often in religious and occult literature and are thought of as powers or faculties of the soul. Some think that the twelve disciples of Jesus represented these powers in that each one had developed one of the twelve powers to a greater extent than others.

In any event, the powers are real enough and can be experienced and developed, as you will discover. In addition to the twelve powers, we will consider another, light, or radiant energy as the source of all. The twelve powers are: Faith, Will, Understanding, Imagination, Enthusiasm, Authority, Love, Wisdom, Joy, Strength, Forgiveness and Life.

I have given classes in these powers on several occasions to a large group of people, and without fail, a number of individuals have had some remarkable experiences that led to complete transformations in their way of life. Healings, changes in employment, improvement in human relations and many other "miracles" have been reported as the result of a new appreciation and working knowledge of these inner powers that make up the kingdom of God in man. Some reported, rather surprised, that improvements were also showing up in the lives of people they did not even care particularly to help. My personal conviction is that these powers are real; that they respond to recognition and exercise, and that they are in reality the nature of God, or the creative spirit in all men.

You are going to enjoy discovering and developing these inner powers for yourself.

DRILL IN THE LIGHT

The following drill is a key to exercising your power to be what you are created to be. As you use the words, the courses of action they describe will open in your consciousness, and eventually the drill will become almost wordless. I am placing the drill here because as you use it, the rest of the book will be more meaningful and helpful, and you will have rich insights of your own to add to whatever I have to share with you.

Here is the first phase of the drill:

I AM THE POWER TO BE

I AM THE POWER TO BE LIGHT

I AM THE POWER TO BE FAITH

I AM THE POWER TO BE WILL

I AM THE POWER TO BE UNDERSTANDING

I AM THE POWER TO BE IMAGINATION

I AM THE POWER TO BE ENTHUSIASM

I AM THE POWER TO BE AUTHORITY

I AM THE POWER TO BE LOVE

I AM THE POWER TO BE WISDOM

I AM THE POWER TO BE JOY

I AM THE POWER TO BE STRENGTH

I AM THE POWER TO BE FORGIVENESS

I AM THE POWER TO BE LIFE

It will be easy for you to memorize these steps in the drill. You will soon feel the flow of energy that gives the drill power in your consciousness.

The second phase in the drill follows:

I AM

I AM LIGHT

I AM FAITH

I AM WILL

I AM UNDERSTANDING

I AM IMAGINATION

I AM ENTHUSIASM

I AM AUTHORITY

I AM LOVE

I AM WISDOM

I AM JOY

I AM STRENGTH

I AM FORGIVENESS

I AM LIFE

You will discover for yourself the changed emphasis in this second part of the drill.

The third phase follows:

I AM ACTION

I AM LIGHT IN ACTION

I AM FAITH IN ACTION

I AM WILL IN ACTION

I AM UNDERSTANDING IN ACTION

I AM IMAGINATION IN ACTION

I AM ENTHUSIASM IN ACTION

I AM AUTHORITY IN ACTION

I AM LOVE IN ACTION

I AM WISDOM IN ACTION

I AM JOY IN ACTION

I AM STRENGTH IN ACTION

I AM FORGIVENESS IN ACTION

I AM LIFE IN ACTION

The final phase of the drill moves you to inspired action—mental, emotional, and in outer ways as well. You may wish to move to a quiet place, get into a comfortable position, relax, and practice the drill until it is established in your consciousness. Repeating the entire drill three times should be sufficient as a beginning.

As you will discover, the first phase of the drill is a revelation of truth, the second phase is the act of claiming it as your own, and the final phase puts it into action. It is not at all unusual for a person to receive flashes of insight even before the drill is completed the first time, and healings, particularly in the mental and emotional nature, are not at all out of the ordinary experience. On the other hand, don't feel discouraged if nothing much seems to happen—at least, you will know the words; the action they describe cannot be far behind!

I hope that after reading each chapter in the remainder of the book you will practice the Drill in the Light. It is in these times of practice and meditation that your own unfoldment receives its greatest thrust and inspiration. As you begin each time of drill, affirm to yourself: "This is going to be the most mind-stretching and heart-lifting drill I have ever experienced." Close your session with the act of praise and thanksgiving described in these words: "I rejoice in my growing ability to carry out the courses of action experienced in this drill."

WHAT'S IN A NAME?

The most important name in the universe is the name of the
Creator. According to the Bible, the name of the Creative Spirit is
I AM! This name is no stranger to us because it is also our
identification tag. We cannot think, feel or speak our identity
without using this name that is above all names. We use it hundreds of times daily and millions of times in a life experience, for
the most part ignorantly and unwisely, unconscious of its infinite
potential in us. I AM is the name of every member of the human
family who has ever lived, who will ever live, including Jesus
Christ. Jesus, however, unlike most men, knew what is in this name.
He knew that I AM is the name of the God nature and potential
in man. He used this name to claim this divine nature for Himself
in courses of inner action described in words like the following: I
AM the light of the world. (He used a variation of this name to
point to the Divinity in all men: YOU ARE the light of the world.)
I AM the way, the truth and the life. I AM the resurrection and the
Life. I AM the door.

WHAT DID JESUS MEAN?

To His statement, "I AM the way, and the truth, and the life,"
He added, "No one comes to the Father, but by me." He also told

His followers that whatever they asked in His name would be done by the Father. Believers in an anthropomorphic god naturally construed this to mean that Jesus, being the Son of God, had a special "pull" with the Father which extended to religious denominations supposedly sponsored by Him, and this gave them the right to dispense (or withhold) privileges to the masses.

A little deeper insight, however, leads one to believe that Jesus had something far more sweeping in mind. He said also: "I AM with you always." Obviously, He was talking of something much greater than His own personality, important and wonderful though that is. I AM means "My true nature is." A little thought will reveal that this is so. I AM is always a statement of being. On a relatively shallow level it identifies the human element in the so-called material or physical world; but in its deeper implications, it identifies the nonmaterial or spiritual elements in us. . . . I AM is the name of God in us.

THE FATHER WITHIN US

Jesus said that He spoke not of Himself, the Father in Him was the source of the words. And as we, too, come into a realization of the true meaning of I AM, we find that it is not our "human" self voicing these words—rather they come from a deeper element of our own being which merely uses our mind and lips to form the words. This Father, or fathering element within us, speaks I AM through us, thus affirming Its individualizing presence and activity of the world.

We will thus readily agree with Jesus' statement that of Himself He did nothing, the Father within does the work.

To put this idea into other words, we can say that the universal expresses through individuality, and that the individual expression, of itself, is powerless—it is dependent upon the universal for its existence and activity. The individual (man) is created to express the universal (God), and is forever dependent on its source for existence, supply and life. Please note, however, that Jesus did not say: "I, of myself, AM nothing." Just as the universal is indispensable to the individual or self-expression—so the individual or self is indispensable to the universal as its instrument of expression.

WHAT'S IN A NAME?

EXPAND YOUR CONSCIOUSNESS

For a little practice in expanding your consciousness of the name I AM, you will find it interesting to rephrase some of the famous I AM statements of Jesus in the following manner: I AM (My True Nature Is) the way, and the truth, and the life. My true nature is the resurrection and the life. My true nature is the door. My true nature is with you always. No one comes to the Father except by Me (My true nature—which is Christ in you, your hope of glory, as St. Paul says it). The next time you practice the Drill in the Light, you can add an extra dimension by using "My true nature is" once or twice instead of I AM.

Amazingly, even the construction of our language carries out this principle of the universal acting through its individual expression or selfhood. The verb "TO BE" symbolizes the infinite potential of the Universal, while its conjugation I AM, YOU ARE, HE IS, SHE IS, IT IS, WE ARE, THEY ARE individualizes that potential.

A little reflection shows that not only do we use the holy name of God when we think, feel or speak our own identity—but we also take that name when we think, feel or speak of our neighbor, both animate and inanimate. Think of the Old Testament prohibitions against taking the name of the Lord in vain and bearing false witness against your neighbor—and you will be led to practicing the Drill in the Light on behalf of your neighbor, using YOU ARE THE POWER TO BE, YOU ARE LIGHT, YOU ARE FAITH IN ACTION, and so on. This expansion of your drill practice will open whole new areas of revelation, thought and feeling to you.

THE SPIRITUAL ELEMENTS OF BEING

As you practice the Drill in the Light, and as you read the rest of this book, you will note that we are concerned primarily with the nonphysical or nonmaterial elements in life. Faith, will, love and the other qualities we are working with are not qualities of matter as we have been accustomed to think of it. I am interested in helping you establish deeper contact and a working relationship with the so-called spiritual elements of being.

Science is revealing that the outer universe of physical form, beginning with the electrons and other "material" elements of the atom is governed by what has been described as "living fields" of force or energy. These "living fields" are similar in nature to the "wave" aspect of light described in Dr. Andrews' letter in Chapter 6. Researchers are finding out that these "living fields" are not controlled by material forms or structures; instead they control and sustain all physical, and probably even mental, forms.

THE DEEPER ENERGIES

These living fields, or wave blueprints, must be controlled, it seems to me, by even deeper and more subtle energies than our scientists have been able to detect. These energies have been named faith, will, enthusiasm, love, wisdom and so on, and they are part of the kingdom of God, the nonphysical, and perhaps even the nonmental, areas of being.

As the individual establishes contact with this deepest part of his own being through processes that have been described as prayer, transcendental meditation, denial and affirmation, the sacraments, and so forth, he releases energies that renew his mental and emotional patterns and eventually transform his physical world, beginning with the structure of his physical body and extending throughout the whole universe of form.

Here, again, science is revealing that even the material elements of the universe are light or energy in concentrated form, which is no doubt the reason that a change in the mental and emotional pattern of an individual affects his whole world. Just as the attitudes, philosophies, fears, moral fiber of a nation determine its handling of material wealth, factories, armaments—so do the attitudes, fears, beliefs and inner make-up of an individual handle the more material elements of his body and world.

Jesus' instructions to seek the inner kingdom and its right use are becoming more meaningful and clear all the time. When a man is in tune with his source and becomes the self-expression of its energies and ideas, he need not be concerned with what he will eat and drink, nor the outer disposition of the atoms of his body or the contents of his bank account—they are controlled by the "living fields" of energy established by his own consciousness.

OUR OWN DOOR

Paul points out that a man's true citizenship is in Heaven. His real identity is in the nonphysical or immaterial areas of being. Jesus said that His kingdom is not of this material world, and that we have to go through a new birth, a washing away of old concepts, before we can enter it. He told his disciples that while He would not pray them out of this world of experience and education, He would pray that they not fall victim to its limitations.

As you use your name, the name of God, I AM to reidentify yourself and to link yourself with the living energies available for self-expression through you, you will be healthier, happier, richer, stronger, more loving, more effective in all your relationships than you have dreamed possible. You, even as I, cannot coast into paradise on anyone else's laurels. Each of us must follow the way pointed out and demonstrated by Jesus Christ, the way of our own individual unfoldment, the door of our own universal I AM.

As you establish a more powerful contact with the unlimited energies of your inner being, as you stir up the wonderful gift that is within you, as the light within expands your power to be, you will really begin to understand in deeper ways the contribution, life and teaching of Jesus Christ. Every manufacturer of note demonstrates his product. Our Creator is no exception. Jesus Christ demonstrated the power and potential built into every man and pointed out that each one was to follow Him in a unique and indispensable demonstration of his own.

What's in a name? Your name? The name of God? I AM? Your answer to these questions will be demonstrated in your life, beginning right now and continuing without interruption for eternity.

6

THE POWER TO BE : LIGHT

When Jesus spoke the words: "I am the light of the world," and "You are the light of the world," He said a spiritual (and what is proving to be a scientific) mouthful. His statement is proving to be literally true. As part of getting this book ready, I wrote to my good friend, Dr. Donald Hatch Andrews, author of the book *The Symphony of Life*, for some suggestions on Light. Dr. Andrews is one of America's respected authorities in the field of chemistry. Here is his reply to my request:

Dear Sig:
I am so happy to get your letter. . . .
From the physical point of view, light is a special manifestation of radiant energy. Light has several physical aspects. Under some circumstances, light appears to behave as if it consisted of waves that are spreading out into space. These are not waves on anything, like waves on water, or waves in anything, like waves of sound in air. They are waves but just one of the fundamental aspects of nature which cannot be described in terms of anything else. Light is light and that is that. Under certain circumstances, light behaves as if it were made up of little compact bundles of energy which travel in individual units rather than as trains of waves. These bundles are called photons.
Since 1923, physicists and chemists have been aware that there is a wave aspect not only to light, but also to various forms of matter. Again, matter can behave as if it were made up of wave trains or it can

behave, under special circumstances, as if it were made up of little bundles to which we give the name, atoms. There are also the electrical forms of matter-energy such as the electron which, again, behaves sometimes like waves and sometimes like particles.

When we deal with collective matter at the most basic level, it appears that the wave aspect is predominant and that the waves intertwine so that we no longer emphasize the atomic aspect but think of the behavior as a whole. Thus, we are led to the logic that it is in the aspect of the whole that we find the deepest reality. It is in the unity of the whole human being, the aspect that guides and governs not only the personality but the more physical aspects that we find the deepest reality. Since we are led to this by the wave aspect, we can think of this inner reality as something closely resembling light. Thus, when we speak of Christ as the Light of the World, we can think of some of this inner light of His spirit as actually present and vibrant within each of us.

THE UNIVERSAL SUBSTANCE

While I don't qualify as a scientist, I cannot help but be thrilled by this scientific confirmation that not only man, but the whole universe and every creature in it, is made of light or radiant energy. The Old Testament of our Bible tells us that the first step in creation is "Let there be light." This "light" or radiant energy is the substance out of which everything in the universe is made; it is the ocean of energy, or God presence, in which we live and move and have our being, as St. Paul pointed out. Light is the substance or creative energy that God, the Creator, is constantly pouring into the universe, into every creature—it is the cosmic energy that not only makes, but runs creation. The Gospel of John points out that this light shines always and that even the darkness of man's ignorance cannot put it out—it is always there, within the reach of each individual, ready for his acceptance and greater expression and experience of it. In a real sense, light is the essence of all—the radiation of God, the Creator, and the substance of man, the creature. It is also possible that in light we find a meeting ground of understanding for the religious and scientific endeavors of man. In a foreword to the book, *The Soul of the Universe*, by Gustaf Stromberg, Mount Wilson astronomer, are these arresting words:

From the turmoil caused by the great discoveries in the science of physics during the last decades two outstanding new principles have emerged. The first is contained in the Quantum Theory and explains the strange fact that both matter and light appear sometimes as particles and sometimes as waves. The second has evolved from the Theory of Relativity and has resulted in a realization that the material universe is a uniform and interrelated whole, that it is a special aspect of a rational Cosmos. . . .

The two principles have also been applied to the age-old problem of the relationship between mind and matter. We can then understand the connection between the chemical and electric processes in the nervous system and the corresponding sensations and feelings. The most startling results of this study are that the individual memory is probably indestructible and that the essence of all living elements is probably immortal. The study leads to the inevitable conclusion that there exists a World Soul or God.

From another field of science, Sir Alister Hardy, Linacre Professor of Zoology at Oxford, who was awarded his Oxford D.Sc. in 1938, was elected a Fellow of the Royal Society in 1940 and was knighted in 1957 for his work in zoology, observed in the book *The Living Stream:* "I have suggested that the power we call God may well have some fundamental link with the process of evolution. In saying this I hope I shall not be thought to be belittling the idea of God; I would rather appear to be saying that the living stream of evolution is as much Divine as physical in nature, which is what I believe" and, "You will see that I am a biological heretic. I believe that the living world is as closely linked with theology as it is with physics and chemistry: that the Divine element is part of the natural process—not strictly supernatural, but paraphysical."

"YOU ARE THE LIGHT OF THE WORLD"

It is certainly not within the range of this book, or of the author's understanding, to detail how the invisible comes into visible form, how light becomes atoms, molecules, organs, creatures and universes, while at the same time remaining "living fields" of energy that control the manifest creation. It is enough for our purpose to know that there is a level of our own being that lies beneath the physical, mental and emotional aspects—that this level is light or radiant energy that contains not only what we are now, but all that we are to be in the infinite "nows" of eternity.

Read the revelations of our scientists with growing excitement, read the Bible, particularly the first chapter of Genesis and the Gospel of John with a sense of adventure, but most important of all, embark on a course of internal research and outer expression, starting with the spiritual and scientific truth that "you are the light of the world," a divine creature of infinite potential. Assume your role in the great processes of creation as an individual expression, soul, or offspring of light, the divine energy, in the assurance that both the spiritual and scientific insights of humanity back you up.

FOUNDATION FOR LIFE

Consider these ideas from the life and teaching of Jesus Christ; use them as the foundation for a new course of action for your own life:

> Meanwhile the disciples besought him, saying, "Rabbi, eat." But he said to them, "I have food to eat of which you do not know." So the disciples said to one another, "Has any one brought him food?" Jesus said to them, "My food is to do the will of him who sent me, and to accomplish his work. Do you not say, 'There are yet four months, then comes the harvest'? I tell you, lift up your eyes, and see how the fields are already white for harvest. He who reaps receives wages, and gathers fruit for eternal life, so that sower and reaper may rejoice together. For here the saying holds true, 'One sows and another reaps.' I sent you to reap that for which you did not labor; others have labored, and you have entered into their labor."

It may well be that the food of which the disciples were ignorant, the fields that are already white for harvest, are the living fields of cosmic energy (light) that the Sower (God) established in the beginning for the reapers (His sons and daughters), and that Sower and reaper are to rejoice together in the next great stage of human unfoldment.

The light is within you—it has always been there. It has always been knocking at the door of your consciousness. The inner light of the Christ Spirit is "actually present and vibrant" within you. Now that its presence within you is verified by competent authority from both religious and scientific fields, it is up to you to become better acquainted with it. You are to assume your own spiritual and scientific responsibility so that you make your contribution to the new world that is breaking through the pages of history, human and divine. Mass evolution has carried the creative process as far as it can—now it is up to individual men and women to become "Co-Creators" as St. Paul puts it.

Sir Alister Hardy writes of the time when "evolution would no longer be guided from outside the species by natural selection, but by a directive activity from within the organism itself. We would see an organism directing its own evolution toward a goal in the future, whatever that might be decided to be." Now that we are transplanting organs of the body, at least thinking about controlling the sex of future children, brainwashing multitudes, and implementing the great scientific discoveries in many fields, we may have to, as some point out, "play God," ready or not. It's not too early to begin our own individual assignment in the thrilling drama now taking place, to seek first of all the inner kingdom, to exercise to its fullest our power to be.

THE MASTER'S KEY

According to the Master of Living, Jesus, the key to exercising our power to be the light of the world is our attention. He pointed out that the eye is the lamp of the body and that if our eye is sound or single, our whole body will be filled with light. Our attention is our inner eye, the door of our consciousness, and whatever gets our attention eventually gets all of us. An individual can give his attention to anything from a bee or flower to an atom, and the secrets he discovers will fill books or even change the course of humanity. As we give our attention to the light of the world, it will yield its secrets.

In the past, we have been double-minded—we have been too concerned with chasing after false gods (outer concerns) to direct our attention to the source. We have failed to discover and utilize the rich ideas of the world of light because "we, like other animals, have our attention fixed on food, shelter and comfort, on defense against our enemies, on our pleasures, and on our petty vanities. . . . In our mind there is a spark of a divine origin which, if not quenched by our selfish desires, may burst into a flame that can illuminate our field of vision and make it possible for us to discern vistas belonging to a greater world." (Gustaf Stromberg, *The Searchers*)

TO FAN THE SPARK

We fan this "spark of a divine origin" into a living flame by giving our attention to it and letting it reveal its nature and potential through us. Since our attention is "word-conditioned" we can direct it through words that we speak aloud or use silently. The following can serve as guides for you until your own consciousness provides others that may be more meaningful and attention catching for you:

Let there be light.

I give my wholehearted attention to the light of the world I am.

I rejoice as the light of the world that I am flows through my attention to fill my conscious and subconscious mind with radiant energy.

Work with these words and the courses of action they contain until you feel a flow of radiant energy. It will be helpful to take a few minutes to sit in a comfortable position, relax, close your eyes, and then speak the words, "Let there be light." Speak them audibly three times; then close your eyes and speak them silently. Now wait expectantly. Remember the words of Jesus: "You are the light of the world." Also remind yourself of the scientific revelation that every atom of your body is made of light, both in the particle form of concentrated energy and the wave patterns that control the so-called material elements. Do not try to force anything to happen. Let the light that is present in every area of your being reveal itself. And it will! Quite often persons who are not familiar with this practice will experience a definite flow of radiant energy the first time—but do not be concerned if nothing much seems to happen immediately.

A NEW DIMENSION

I remember working with a fine man for weeks in counseling and daily prayer. He came to see me often, and his report was invariably: "I tried hard every day, but nothing happened." Then one day he came in rather sheepishly and said: "Today it happened. I guess I stopped trying, and suddenly there it was—an inner glow. I really can't describe it, but I know it's real." The important thing is to keep on. The light is there, vibrant and ready to reveal its presence and energy.

Once you become conscious of this inner light, a subtle and marvelous change takes place in you. Oh, you don't suddenly sprout wings and flit from place to place, but you become aware of a new dimension of your own being; you don't become upset quite so easily or stay upset so long; you begin to do your own thinking and to have inner revelations of your own. Many who are getting acquainted with this inner light report that they find sudden insights into the meaning of scripture flashing into their minds, and that they find answers to questions that had been bothering them for a long while. Others say that members of their family or friendship circle sense a change for the better in them. A nurse friend told me that after a "drill in the light" three of her patients said that when she walked into their rooms it was as if a light had been turned on. I think that this is exactly what happens. A light is turned on—in the mind, heart and body. Every atom, according to Dr. Andrews, has a point of light as its nucleus. It is no doubt true that every cell is a unit of light, or radiant energy—and that the body is itself a temple of light, potentially, if not in expression yet.

THE CURRENT OF LIGHT

I have had some interesting and inspiring experiences during counseling sessions. On at least two or three occasions I have become highly conscious of a current of light flowing through the person to whom I was listening or speaking. At least once, the light was so clear and strong that I almost forgot what I was doing to watch it. When I spoke words of faith, hope and life the light current would flow in a straight path, but the moment the woman I was counseling turned her attention again to her agonizing problem, the light turned at a sharp angle and disappeared from my consciousness—I say consciousness, because I can't say that I really saw the light through my physical eyes, but I was deeply conscious of it.

It would seem to me that the light that was designed to flow into radiant expression through this person was instead diverted into the problem which was causing her so much distress. I might add that I am known as a "hardheaded Swede" and I am not given to "seeing things." I am convinced that the light within is real!

FULFILLING THE BIBLICAL PROMISE

The promise of the Bible is that those who follow Jesus Christ will no longer walk in darkness but will come into the light. Moving from darkness to light is a gradual process. Revelations of truth and light come readily—putting them into practice takes longer and proves a greater challenge. You can encourage and accelerate the process with words such as these:

> *I praise and give thanks for my growing ability to keep my attention on the light that fills my whole being with radiant energy.*

> *I praise and give thanks for my growing ability to individualize the power to be the light of the world.*

Become so conscious of the light that it profoundly affects every area of your being—the mental, emotional and physical. Meditate on the light regularly. The secrets of the kingdom of atomic energy were not uncovered through casual investigation. The kingdom of light holds even greater potential for mankind; as a matter of fact, we can say that atomic energy is only part of the kingdom of light—its deeper and more important elements are still to be brought into expression in the experience of men.

Your research into the nature of light is just as important as any project that is going in any scientific laboratory anywhere in the world. Stir up your attention, your interest, your thinking with light-filled words like these:

> *My delighted and enlightened thinking permits the light of the world I am to fill mind, heart and body with radiant, stimulating, refreshing energy.*

You are waking yourself up—or you are awakening to your radiant, light-filled Self. Give this inner light at least half as much attention as you give your aches and pains, problems, fears and unhappinesses—and you will be a miracle in your world. Move boldly into the dark spots of mind, heart and body with sweeping affirmations of light like the following:

> *The light of the world I am flows through my wholehearted attention to wipe the darkness of fear, resentment, doubt, procrastination and inertia out of my conscious and subconscious mind.*

> *The light of the world I am flows through my delighted attention to wipe the darkness of congestion, weakness, fatigue and disease out of my body.*

If these are merely words to begin with, fine. Remember the words of Jesus: "You are the light of the world. Let your light shine." Think through the words of James: "Do not be deceived, my beloved brethren. Every good endowment and every perfect gift is from above, coming down from the Father of lights with whom there is no variation or shadow due to change." Every gift—health, prosperity, success, spiritual understanding, good government, good human relations—you name it—comes through the activity of life, the light of the world that you truly are. Get to know that inner light, your own radiant self, the Christ in you. Woo it. Think about it. Feel it. Speak of it and to it. Go to bed with it. Sleep with it. Get up with it. Drink with it. Eat with it. Work with it. Pray, walk, run, drive in the light of your awakening Selfhood!

7

THE POWER TO BE:
FAITH

Faith is our spiritual capital. The dividends it returns to us depend on the investment we make of it. "Faith gives substance to our hopes, and makes us certain of realities we do not see," says our Bible. Dr. George Lamsa, famed Aramaic scholar, translates this well-known passage from the letter to the Hebrews in this way: "Now faith is the substance of things hoped for, as it was the substance of things which have come to pass; and it is the evidence of things not seen." The function of faith is to make things that are unseen real and substantial to us. It is the highly specialized energy that gives a mental, emotional and physical body of expression to whatever we believe in. Not only does it bring forth the good things we hope for and desire, when misdirected it brings forth and makes substantial the things worried about, resented and feared. Faith has always been a part of man's divine make-up and experience. Every project was faith once, and every project of the future will be faith first. It is the energy that has given a mental, emotional, physical, social, financial, political, economic and international body of expression to what men have believed.

Faith, individualized in and operating through man, has built his mental attitudes, his factories and businesses, his churches and educational institutions, his hospitals and libraries, his ghettoes and concentration camps, his wars and his efforts at peace. Faith, operating through man, will build the mental attitudes and shape the outlines of the universe of the future. Faith in an outer god has produced churches and religious institutions; faith in the light within will produce individuals who are consciously becoming temples of the living God.

PUTTING FAITH TO WORK

Faith is put to work through a process called believing. Believing is much more than mere intellectual assent to a truth or proposition, although this may well be the beginning. Believing is a consistent activity that keeps faith on the job until it has made an unseen reality substantial by giving it a mental, emotional and physical body of expression. Faith can be used negatively or positively, constructively or destructively. Fear is an emotion aroused by faith in something harmful, destructive or evil, and it produces a whole chain of unhappy events in the mental, physical and social body of mankind.

Faith goes where our attention is centered, and it always works perfectly to bring forth what we really believe. In counseling, I have found it both startling and helpful to ask someone who has just finished a long recital of his problems a question like this: "You really have a strong and active faith in your problems, don't you? Are you willing to put that much faith into the power that can solve your problems?" Often this approach works something of a miracle in the consciousness of the person concerned, although there are those who consciously or unconsciously want to hang on to their difficulties a bit longer. According to the records, Jesus often asked people if they really wanted to be healed, or if they believed He could heal them—and then He told them that their prayers would be answered according to their faith.

RESIST NOT EVIL

Man has built a stubborn faith in the dark side of his nature—his sins, his unworthiness, his guilts, his resentments, his fears, his separation from God. Experts in misdirecting faith have been on the job for centuries. Well-meaning in many instances, but unaware of the true facts of man's divine nature, they have used many weapons to prey on his ignorance, his superstitions and his gullibility. A friend of mine once told me in jest (I hope) that "if ignorance were bliss, you'd be a blister!" Man's ignorance of his true nature has blistered his soul, his mind and his body with inner and outer wars. There is no doubt that there is plenty wrong with man's behavior, but he will never rise above it until he begins to put his faith into what is right with him—the inner light, radiation and activity of God, his Creator.

Jesus told his followers to "resist not evil," but if his advice was heard it was soon ignored. Attacking evil soon became the chief occupation of organized religion; an unyielding faith in the reality of evil, the devil and the sinful nature of man became a "must," and the divine potential of man as the image of God was pretty much lost in the scuffle.

To resist evil, to focus attention on it, is to reproduce it, and organized religion has been successful, not in the way it intended, of course, because by the admission of its own leaders there is more sin in the world today than ever before! Faith always reproduces what we believe in, that to which we give our wholehearted attention. Faith in evil produces fear of punishment, and fear in all its forms is the main reason man is sick, unhappy and warlike. To try to frighten man into being good, to instill the "fear" of God in him is to wreck his usefulness and potential as the light of the world.

THE RIGHT USE OF FAITH

If religion is to save man, it must save him from the effort of his own fears, ignorance and misconceptions, and to do this it must teach the right use of faith. Man can never be what he is designed to be—the image of God, the light of the world—until he puts his faith into his own potential of good. "Fear not, only believe," is the inspired instruction of the Master Teacher. Believe in God, the Universal Good, and Me, Christ, the individual expression of the Universal Good, present and ready for action in every man, is a message and course of action that must be accepted and carried out by all. To put faith into the light of the world in man is not to condone or encourage past inadequate actions, but to lay the groundwork for inspired action in the present and future.

FROM DARKNESS TO LIGHT

To switch our faith from the dark side of life and the dark side of our own nature to the light takes boldness and persistence. Faith is always a moving into the unknown, a moving from familiar if uncomfortable paths, a moving into uncharted ways and experiences. A start can be made simply enough. The use of faith-filled, confident words builds the blueprint in consciousness for continued action. Even if the words seem unfamiliar at first, use the staying power of faith until they become a permanent part of your system of thought and feeling.

The following words can help you make the switch:

Beginning right now and continuing without interruption, I switch my faith from darkness to light. I exercise my power to be faith in action. I believe that I am the light of the world, and my faith makes that light real and substantial to me.

Remember that in working with faith you are using a substance—the substance out of which the things you hoped for (or feared) in the past have been made, and your present faith is the evidence of things not yet come into visibility, things that are now invisible, in the treasure chest of your expectancy. We are now learning that the substance of all things, visible and invisible, is energy. Some of this energy is bottled up in patterns of thought and feeling, some of it is in physical form—but most of it is free and uncommitted to any form.

THE FUNCTIONS OF FAITH

Faith is that highly specialized energy that works in and on every area of the energy or light reservoir. It breaks up old patterns in the mental, emotional and physical realm, it establishes new patterns in the "living fields" of energy in which all form exists, and it lays hold of uncommitted light and gives it a mental, emotional and physical body of expression. The great achievers of the world are the great believers of the world. Join them right now by putting your faith to work and keeping it on the job until the light of the world you are becomes a substantial, living reality in and through you.

The writers of the Bible looked upon faith as an outstanding virtue and power. All the great figures are regarded as living examples of faith in action—from Moses to Jesus, they put the cosmic energies to work for good and mighty deeds through exercising their faith. Job, in his more unhappy aspects, is an example of the wrong use of faith, for he moans in his deepest misery that what he feared had come upon him.

BAD HABITS OR GOOD?

I heard once of a man who asked for prayers for healing. He had quite a sense of humor and he said that he had been ill for years and that he had had so many operations he was afraid to go to a doctor because he had nothing left to remove or operate on. He said he felt almost like a plumber's helper because his inner organs and equipment had been disconnected and reconnected so much. The counselor to whom he was talking asked him if he really wanted to be healed. When he had received the assurance that such was indeed the case, the counselor said: "Well, then let's get our faith out of the diseases and operations and put it into the healing power of God." The man agreed, and after a time of prayer, left. That evening the counselor was entering his apartment when the telephone rang. The excited voice of the man seeking healing came over the wire: "Do you know, Dr. ——, there's one operation I forgot completely to tell you about this afternoon."

Faith operates in the direction we give it, and when we permit it to fall into bad habits, it always delivers in accordance with our prevailing expectations.

On a happier note, I remember a young woman who used to come in for counseling. She won't mind my telling her story because she has asked me to use it wherever and whenever it may be of help. Every time she came into my office, she would say: "Sig, get out your box of Kleenex. I am ready for another good cry." And then she would sob out her tale of woe. We prayed together and discussed many of the ideas and courses of action described in this book, and I felt there was gradual improvement.

I left the city for another assignment and did not see this young lady for a number of years; but one day she came into my office, and I could hardly believe my eyes. She was absolutely radiant, and she told me that her whole life had been completely transformed. She said she could hardly wait for the new day and the wonderful experiences life was bringing to her. It was no longer necessary, she joyously assured me, for her to outline or try to figure out just what she needed—she was quite willing to leave that to God. She told me that her prayers consisted mostly of one affirmative statement that she had fashioned from her study, counseling and experience. Here it is: "Miracle follows miracle. Wonders never cease. My expectancy is of the good. Come on something!"

As Jesus, and others have pointed out, our Heavenly Father or life itself, knows our needs before we get around to asking, and when our faith permits it, will pour good into expression in our world.

TARGETS OF FAITH

Faith is not designed to work on some outer god or distant giver of good—faith is the energy that can change the mental and emotional patterns of your own consciousness. As far as you are concerned, your own beliefs, thoughts and feelings are always the targets of your faith. When your faith changes them sufficiently, miracles are on their way, and you are always the miracle that happens, whether it appears as a healing, guidance, supply or any other form of good. Let your faith work until it changes your prevailing attitudes of mind for the better, and you will have the inner evidence of an outer change for good that is already on the way.

If we had the proper instruments, we would probably see and say that your faith had changed the vibration rate of the "living fields" of energy that govern the so-called material aspects of your life. Since these living fields are present in your mind and heart, in every atom and cell of your body, in every atom and operation of your business, in every breath you draw and every word you speak, in every relationship you have, it is easy to believe that faith is the power to transform your life, from the inside out.

OTHER MIRACLES

In hypnotic experiments we see something of the powers of the unconscious or responsive energies of the self. A hypnotized "weakling" responding to suggestion becomes a tower of strength. He performs feats that would be utterly impossible to him if his own conscious mind were in control of his body.

Faith works miracles in another way. It "unhypnotizes" the one who uses it. Faith frees the mind that is caught in the grip of limitation; it vitalizes the living fields of energy that have sunk to the low vibration of inertia, disease and congestion; it stimulates the circulation of good in the world governed by the one using it. Usually it takes an emergency of one kind or another to unleash the unused energies that are available for self-expression through us. Faith, consciously used, releases these cosmic energies and permanently lifts the living level of our experience.

AN EXERCISE IN FAITH

Faith can be defined and explained in enough ways to fill the books of a great library, but the only way to know what it is is simply to put it to work. "Faith without works is dead." Prove it in your own consciousness and life, and faith will be yours by right of experience.

In addition to the Drill in the Light, you may want to exercise your faith in some of the following courses of action:

The targets of my faith are my own attitudes, thoughts and feelings.

I have a dynamic, miracle-working faith that unhypnotizes my mind and frees it from the grip of limitation.

I believe in God and in my own divine selfhood until my faith makes them real and substantial to me.

I exercise a powerful faith that revitalizes the "living fields" of energy that govern the material elements of my life.

My growing faith stimulates the circulation of good in my world.

My joyous faith releases the cosmic energies that are available for self-expression through me.

I exercise an adventurous faith in the unlimited potential of my own being.

I believe in the kingdom of God within, and my faith makes it real and active in me.

The foregoing, coupled with the Drill in the Light, provide the foundation for an exercise in faith. Be ready to move into exercises of your own. The purpose of this book is to help you to become spiritually independent, and only you can decide when you are ready to move out under your own guidance and inspiration. Dare to believe in yourself, beginning right now!

TAKE YOURSELF JOYOUSLY

As you continue to keep your faith where it belongs, you may find that the ideas in the next words give you a lift:

It is easy, natural and profitable to believe in the truth of being. My faith in the light of the world that I am (and that my neighbor is, too!) pays rich dividends in every area of living. The light of the world that I am fills my mind, heart, body, business and outer activities.

Learn to take yourself joyously. Remember that Jesus taught that His yoke is easy and His burden light, and that He pointed out that to seek and find the inner kingdom of God (light) is the most profitable undertaking we can enter because doing this provides for our every need as well. Get out of the rut of conditioned and habitual thinking. Use words that stimulate your faith, lift your vision and energize your mental and emotional processes of self-expression.

FAITH IN ACTION

Faith in the light, the inner kingdom of good, dissolves the worry habit which victimizes most of humanity in one form or another. Worry is fear in action. Confidence is faith in action, and as you continue to believe in the light, old habits of worry and anxiety are lifted right out of your experience. Worry is a habit that once established sustains itself—it seeks out its own targets and constantly drains the energy of the one who is its victim.

Even after the problem that may have started the habit of worry is solved, the old habit often persists.

It is difficult and almost impossible to overcome worry by a direct attack, but the establishment of the confidence habit will replace worry. I have seen the confidence, faith-in-action, therapy work miracles in many, many people. In several instances before the worry habit was finally dissolved, both men and women have come in with rather sheepish expressions on their faces and in their minds and said in substance: "Today the only thing I could find to worry about was the fact that I no longer seem worried about anything!"

When worry, fear in action, occupies our minds, it is difficult to be healthy, happy, prosperous, effective contributors to the well-being of the world we live in. As your faith makes the light within real and substantial and active in you, daily miracles will flow into expression through you. Every miracle has its roots in the invisible, the infinite, inexhaustible, radiant energy (light) of the nonmaterial world that is always available, always within the reach of your faith. Your faith-in-action is making you the confident, radiant self-expression of the light of the world that you are truly are!

THE POWER TO BE:
WILL

The will of God is the irresistible urge of universal good to find self-expression in and through its creation.

The will of God is the cosmic energy that flows through the universe urging every atom, cell and creature to higher levels of performance.

The will of God surges through all creation in evolutionary and revolutionary waves of progress, constantly breaking up old patterns of limitation, initiating and fulfilling new designs of good.

The will of God is the purpose, determination and desire of the Universal Creative Spirit to find ever-greater self-expression through creatures of expanding potential, of which man is the most expandable, and often seemingly the most reluctant.

The will of God is the triumph of love over hate, light over darkness, life over death, strength over weakness, joy over unhappiness, abundance over lack, health over disease, unity over separation, peace over war, wisdom over ignorance, forgiveness over condemnation, freedom over bondage.

The will of God is man's slowly unfolding consciousness of the unity of the universe, the brotherhood of humanity, and of his own infinite potential as the expression of that universal will of good.

Without will man is nothing. With a selfish sense of will man is a devil. With the universal sense of will man becomes the god he is created to be!

The will of God is the impulse behind and in the whole creative process. The creative process gives expression to the nature of the Creator, and it is the will of the Creator that works constantly to sustain and stimulate its instruments and functions of self-expression.

THE TROUBLE WITH NEGATIVE WILLPOWER

On the "human" level of experience, it is easy to see that it is the will of the individual, his basic intent, purpose, determination, that gives direction and energy to his instruments and functions of expression. If he feels isolated and separated from his Creator, his fellowmen and his world, his will is selfish, egotistical, fearful and destructive. He becomes what we term a "willful" person, and he exercises his will on every element in his world. We can read his willful intent in his face, in his self-concern, in his mental and emotional reactions, in his handling of money and other goods, and in his lack of concern for and understanding of others. A willful man is always busy trying to feather his own nest, protecting his own limited interests, and subtly or violently trying to get the rest of humanity to conform to his own concepts of what is right or wrong. Naturally, man's consciousness is reflected in his religious, social, political and international activities—so we see institutions and governments carrying out the policies determined by the will of the individuals who are their members and supporters.

CONCEPTS OF GOD

It is natural, too, that man's will should show up in his concepts of God—and for centuries a willful god has been diligently worshiped and served by so-called "civilized" elements of humanity. God was portrayed as an outer deity, a higher authority who imposed or tried to impose his will on creation, a creator who so botched up the job of creating his chief creature, man, that he got completely out of control. In order to regain control of man, to impose the divine will on him, the creator was supposed to inflict disease, punishment, suffering and finally death—a death that was presumably the door to a world of even greater punishment and suffering for the nonconformists and nonreligious. Perhaps as a side effect, or maybe for a little practice, the will of this god included suffering, disease and death even for the select few who could meet the rigid specifications of particular creeds and doctrines of belief, always with the promise of better things ahead in the paradise that waited for the "saved."

The "saved" were reportedly those who believed that Jesus Christ is the only begotten son of God, that His bloody death on the cross somehow appeased the anger of the ruler of the universe, and that certain creeds and codes of behavior were the will of God for the earthly tour of duty. Since the sacrifice on Calvary did not seem to make much of a dent in the will of God—at least, men continued to suffer, become sick and die—paradise was once again moved off to a distant place and time, and a "good Christian" was to accept the will of God and resign himself patiently to the suffering that it included.

JESUS' TEACHING ABOUT GOD

The teaching of Jesus Christ, of course, reveals that the outraged, vengeful, outer deity exists only in the misconceptions of men's beliefs and fearful minds. On the other hand, man has to serve the concepts he entertains in his mind and heart, and as long as he holds an inferior view of the will of God he must live with it. According to the teaching of Christ, God is changeless. The Creative Spirit does not move up and down like some supernatural yo-yo on the string of human reaction and will in Its attitudes toward men. The divine goodness is poured out without distinction on all men, the good and the bad, the just and the unjust, the wise and the ignorant, the religious and the irreligious. Like the sunshine and the rain, the divine will does not withhold good from any creature (including man) because of its behavior, code of ethics, religious doctrine or social creed. The divine will, or intent, keeps the stream of good flowing to and through all its creation, and the suffering so often attributed to the will of God has its roots in quite another source—man's unwillingness to accept the will of God as his own! Man's problems and suffering come from his own slowness in accepting his power to be the will of God in individual expression, from his own reluctance to be reborn into the light of the world and to enter the spiritual dimensions of his own being. The Gospel of John points out that all who receive Jesus Christ, who believe in His name (or method), receive power to become children of God—"who were born, not of blood nor of the will of the flesh, nor of the will of man, but of God."

THE DIVINE IMPERATIVE

Many counselors and doctors of the mind find that the "will of God" is often put forth as a real obstacle to healing, individual initiative and personal progress and unfoldment in the lives of those they seek to help. "The will of God" is used as both scapegoat and escape hatch. It is often blamed for everything from incurable diseases to the weather and the political and economic climate. Seldom is it recognized as an infinite power to be tapped and brought to bear in the experiences of everyday living—a cosmic energy to be individualized and expressed through everyone. I have seen men and women healed, mentally and emotionally, and even physically, right before my eyes when they learned that the will of God is always good, always healing in its action, always working for the highest good of everyone concerned in any situation, always triumphant when given free rein.

We can now lay aside forever that tired, old concept of the will of God as undesirable, destructive of peace and happiness—a power that inflicts punishment of one kind or another upon us. The will of God is the divine imperative, the cosmic urge for self-expression, the irresistible impulse of the light to shine, the joyous invitation of the Infinite, persuading man to come up higher in thought, feeling and action. The will of God, individualized in man, becomes his expanding desire for good, first for himself, but eventually and inevitably, for all humanity—and indeed for all creation! The will of God is the highest motivation of the human spirit—the "power behind the throne" of every desire for individual and universal good. The will of God is the unshakable guarantee that underwrites the whole creative process and assures the success of all its enterprises, with man holding top priority.

SURRENDER TO GOD'S WILL

The individual taps the power of the will of God by surrendering to it! Jesus surrendered to the will of God in the Garden of Gethsemane and then was moved through the crucifixion to the triumph of the resurrection—the demonstration of life over death. Jesus was much too enlightened to believe that the will of God meant just suffering and death—He told His followers that He knew the command (or will) of God is eternal life—He saw that the will of God is the overcoming and elimination of suffering and death from the consciousness of mankind through the greater expression of life. He also realized that the only way to make this great demonstration was to surrender to the will that made it possible, and so we have the record of His words: "Not my will, but thine, be done," to serve as models for our own inner work in consciousness.

Conventional religious thought holds that the agony in the Garden of Gethsemane came through Jesus' contemplation of the suffering and death that confronted Him, and while there were certainly elements of this state of mind involved, it is only part of the story. He was concerned with an even greater stride upward in understanding—the complete triumph of life over death, the extinction of the human concept of existence, and the coming forth of a whole, new creature, not shaped by the will of man, but moved by the will of God. Man usually gives up his most revered limitations, particularly his "religious" ones, with howls of anguish, and Jesus had to overcome this tendency in His Own consciousness, the only place of overcoming, since He had voluntarily taken on the limitations (sins) of the world.

He realized that the only way to complete His mission was to tap the overcoming power of the will of God, and He did, with results that are only barely penetrating the consciousness of mankind 2000 years later. Through His surrender to the will of God, Jesus became the "first fruits" of all who had been asleep to their life potential, or as Teilhard de Chardin intimates, the point "Omega—God-made-Man" prototype of the new humanity, a race of gods destined to rule the earth, and apparently a considerable part of the outer universe as well.

THE GREATER LIGHT

While there are probably few whose consciousness can comprehend the full import of the resurrection of Jesus Christ from the dead habits of human thought and experience, all who choose can follow Him in a daily experience of surrendering to the will of God. As they experience the resurrection from lesser habits of limitation, the way will be opened for greater resurrections to take place and eventually, event by event, the light will dawn in greater glory for each one who is willing to make the effort.

The worm in the cocoon has no understanding of the butterfly that will soon take flight, even though elements of the winged creature and its design are already present (and active) in the seemingly imprisoned forerunner. With us, too, it is likely that the radiant, light-filled creature we are to become is apparent only as vague and fleeting stirrings and desires for a richer life taking place in the as yet unconscious depths of being. As Teilhard de Chardin points out, man is but the embryo of what he is destined to become; so even if the path ahead is not too clear, we can make a start with the light we have now, knowing that as we move ahead in faith, willing to surrender to the will of our Creator, greater light is on the way.

YOU AND THE WILL OF GOD

The ideas contained in the statements that follow, combined with the Drill in the Light, can open a rich experience in living for you if you are willing to put them to work. Do not let the words tie you to a rigid format. Use the words and ideas that appeal to you, or even better, let your rich consciousness fire its own dynamic courses of action into your mind and heart. You who read are the message of this book, and the sooner you make this discovery, the more rapid will be your progress. "Think on these things":

The will of God is the cosmic urge for self-expression.

The will of God, individualized in me, is my rapidly expanding desire for universal good.

The will of God is the desire of Infinite love, life, joy and wholeness for self-expression through me and the rest of humanity.

The will of God is that I let my light shine in a way that glorifies its Source (the Father within) and inspires my neighbor to take up the same activity.

The will of God is that I live up to my highest potential at all times and in all situations.

The will of God is that I choose life instead of death, love instead of hate, health instead of sickness, prosperity instead of poverty, peace instead of war, joy instead of unhappiness.

The will of God is that I love the Lord my God . . . and my neighbor as myself.

The will of God is that I expand my desire for good so that it includes all humanity, those of every race, creed, nation and color.

The will of God is that I be a successful human being, ever unfolding more of my spiritual potential and capacity.

The will of God is that I be a successful man or woman, boy or girl.

The will of God is that I be successful in all enterprises, for the blessing and benefit of all mankind.

The will of God is that I be prosperous and generous in all things, mentally, emotionally and outwardly as well.

The will of God is that I circulate the good, inner and outer, that has been entrusted to me.

The will of God is that I shall come to know and appreciate the divine nature in me and in my neighbor, and in all creation.

The will of God is that I shall come to know and experience eternal life, beginning right now.

AN ADVENTURE OF SURRENDER

Books could be written defining the will of God, but together we have garnered enough information to embark on an adventure of surrender to the mightiest will in the universe, the will of its Creator. Let the words that follow direct your mind and heart into the actions they describe:

With a growing sense of confidence, delight and expectancy, I surrender to the will of God.

I surrender to the will of God with a joyous abandon that accelerates the breakup of old habits of limitation.

I surrender to the will of God because I want to do it.

I surrender to the will of God because I am fed up with limited, willful patterns of behavior and experience.

I surrender to the will of God because I want to become the light of the world that I am.

I surrender to the will of God—the will of light, the will of love, the will of life, the will of joy, the will of success and accomplishment, the will of circulation and sharing, the will of peace, the will of abundance.

With a delicious sense of freedom, I pray: "Not my will, but thine be done."

As the will of God expands its operation in and through you, expect great things to happen in your everyday experience and activity. Remember that this good, old earth is the proving ground for all of us. The will of God does not remove us from the necessary activities of human relationships, business, political or social operations, religious, racial or international stress (Jesus told His disciples He would not pray them out of this world, but would give them a hand in overcoming their limited views of its role in their unfoldment)—the will of God equips us to be more effective partners in the business of living. Prove this truth in the world in which you live, work and grow right now.

CARRY THE GOSPEL WITH YOU

A businessman came to me and said that I had startled him right out of his limitations by stating in a class that it was the will of God that every business and its owner should be prosperous and successful, so that they could make the right kind of contribution to the society that supported them. He reminded me that I had said that an unsuccessful man or business was a drain on humanity and that life would not tolerate either of them indefinitely any more than it would permit an unprofitable species to continue. He told me that he had been laboring under the burden of believing that it was impossible for a rich man to enter the kingdom of heaven and that if he were successful he was somehow compromising the future of his soul. He said he had been struck by the inconsistency of his being told by the Church on one hand that wealth was wrong or "evil" and its insistence on the other hand that he should constantly increase his pledge of financial assistance for its support.

But there the matter remained until he learned that the wealthy young man who was unable to follow Jesus because he could not give up his possessions was blocked not by the things he owned but by his attitudes toward them. The young man did not really "possess" his possessions, they "possessed" him, and he had a tough time going anywhere, let alone to Heaven, because of his dependence on the things that he felt he owned.

The will of God does not lead to the poorhouse—it teaches us how to handle our material (and spiritual) possessions for the universal good. Jesus told the rich young man to sell his goods and give to the poor, which is a graphic way of telling him to change his attitudes and heal his poor states of mind so that he could become a profitable agent for the will of good (God). The disciples were then told by Jesus that while a rich man could not do it on his own, God could handle the matter. My businessman friend told me that his whole attitude toward his work was changed, everything was improving, and he was carrying the "gospel" to his customers, and even his competitors.

THE TRIUMPH OF FAITH

The will of God is not just "spiritual" or "religious"; it finds rich application in every area of human experience. Myrtle Fillmore, co-founder of the Unity movement, had been told by expert opinion that she was the victim of an incurable disease and had only a few months to live. She and her husband attended a lecture given by a leader in the "New Thought" field and learned that she was a child of God, and that the will of God was health, not disease. She decided that her inheritance was from the will of God, not from the will of man, and that she could be healed. She has written how in times of prayer and meditation she went mentally to the cells and organs of her body, asking forgiveness for the false concepts she had held of them, and informing them that their natural state was radiant health. She was healed, and out of her experience grew the prayer work of Silent Unity, an organization known around the world for its prayer activity, based on the principle that the will of God for man is health, prosperity, peace, happiness, spiritual understanding and everything good.

"Let your light shine." Be willing to let the will of God operate in your daily living—in your business, your profession, your work, your home, your relations with others. Be willing to let the will of God operate your mind, heart and body. As the divine will works its miracle of daily demonstration and resurrection, you will be readied for even greater miracles of understanding and experience. Surrender to the will of the Creator who designed and produced you for the purpose of giving self-expression to Its nature of infinite good!

9

THE POWER TO BE:
UNDERSTANDING

There is something in us that cries out for understanding. We are always wanting to know "what makes things tick." We want to know how to do things, how to make improvements in the way we live. A few years ago I visited Africa on a special assignment and several of my new-found friends said that they were most interested in the "know-how" of the citizens of my country. They (my African friends) felt they had plenty of natural and human resources but needed to know how to use them more effectively. The Bible urges that with all our getting we get understanding, and reportedly the wisest man in history, Solomon, pleased God by asking for it.

WHAT DO WE SEEK?

The understanding we seek is more than intellectual knowledge; it is more than the secondhand knowledge that books, teachers or institutions can hand down to us—it is the working knowledge that comes only from direct experience. It is the "know-how" that grows through participation in the activity we seek to understand. To know that we are the light of the world is only a beginning. To understand that light, we must experience it. Jesus said that if we live in the revelation (light) He brought, we would come to know (experience) the truth, and the truth would then set us free!

To live in the light, to experience the light, is to gain a working knowledge or understanding of it, and then the light of truth sets us free from all the unenlightened habits, attitudes and states of mind that have held us in bondage. When we start exercising the power to be understanding, we engage in a growing, unfolding activity that involves all the elements of our being, both visible and invisible, material and nonmaterial. The light of the world that we are flows through mind, heart, body, business, society and all areas of our outer world.

CHANGING CONSCIOUSNESS

As understanding begins in our mind we may say: "Ah, at last I see the light," or "The light of truth is dawning in me," and our consciousness begins to change. We spend more time thinking the thoughts of light, wholeness, joy, peace and strength and we begin to be freed from the unenlightened thoughts of separation, fear, and other forms of limitation. As the understanding flows through our emotional, physical, social and external nature—the process of enlightenment continues to free us from the unenlightened bondage of our past.

One of the most thrilling parts of being in my particular work is to see the miracles that take place in those who are discovering, trusting and experiencing their own "inner light." As they come to realize more and more that success or failure in living are the products of their own understanding (or consciousness), and that they can always improve their understanding, a new world opens for them. They pass from the theories and concepts of intellectual knowledge about the truth into a working knowledge or understanding of the light of the world.

LET THE LIGHT SHINE

When we are willing (desiring, accepting and expecting) to let the light of the world shine through us, we increase our understanding or working knowledge of it. When we are willing to let the light shine, we are doing the will of light because its nature or purpose is to shine, to dissolve the darkness of limitation, and to set us free to express more of its infinite nature in us. Jesus said that we could test the validity of His teaching by doing the will of God. Once we accept the light of the world as the truth of our being and let it shine or operate in us, we will soon know the truth of the teaching—whether it comes from the Source of all, or whether it is just someone's opinion. We can never know whether we are on the pathway of truth until that truth is unfolding through us.

I have had people come to me and ask if they could follow the inner light and still retain their church membership in some denominational group—they just did not want to take any chances on being forced to face the "final judgment" in the event the traditional concepts were right.

DEPEND ON THE LIGHT WITHIN

Until we are ready to depend on the light within, we are never certain of our understanding, or of any teaching—we constantly run from church to church, teacher to teacher, doctrine to doctrine, hoping in this way to find verification of our beliefs or doubts. And, of course, we can never be satisfied or sure until the light, itself, becomes the substance of our understanding. As our working knowledge of the light increases, we have less need to run elsewhere for verification. We will have a deepening understanding bcause we are doing the will of God by letting light shine in a way that reveals its source, the kingdom or nature of God within. This inner light reveals the nature of God, just as the rays of the sun reveal the nature of the sun. Light in all its facets—and they are infinite—is the nature of God in operation, and man is the instrument designed to give it unlimited expression.

THE BREATH OF THE ALMIGHTY

We begin with our present understanding of light, regardless of how limited our understanding may be, in the assurance that it will grow through practice. Perhaps an idea from the Old Testament of our Bible will be as helpful to you as it has been to me. Here it is:

> Truly, there is a spirit in men; and the breath of the Almighty gives them understanding. (Job 32:8 Lamsa)

This spirit is the inner light, "present and vibrant," and the breath or activity of it (the Almighty) gives understanding, or working knowledge.

The process of breathing contains the secret of life. If we feel that it is only a physical activity, we miss its real importance. We are warned not to take the man whose "breath is in his nostrils" into account—man is much more than a physical being, and breathing is much more than an action of the nostrils and lungs. Breathing is the process by which the universal individualizes and expresses its infinite light or radiant energy.

The "breath of the Almighty" corresponds to the waves of light that our scientists detect flowing into the living fields of energy that support and maintain the so-called material world. This divine breathing or wave of radiant energy transmits revelation and ideas to the mind of man, love and joy to man's emotional nature, life and health to man's body, prosperity and success to man's affairs, and peace and harmony to man's world—all according to his understanding or working knowledge of it.

WHY DO WE BREATHE?

We can learn much from a study of our breathing. It is easy to see that in breathing we individualize the universal atmosphere that surrounds the earth—in our earth experience, there is nothing more universal than air, or nothing more individual and personal than breathing. Breathing reveals our unity with all other creatures (atoms, plants, animals)—when we breathe in, we are drawing on an element to which all have contributed and when we breathe out we are ourselves making a contribution to the universal atmosphere. This reveals the law of "giving and receiving" or the principle of circulation on which all life form is dependent. While we all must breathe to live, we all determine in great degree the depth and intensity of our breathing, and we can always improve our understanding of it by practicing better methods of breathing.

It seems quite likely that breathing is the process that connects our nonmaterial elements of being with the material parts. We enter our physical body at birth with an excited breath, and we lay aside our body with our last breath. It is doubtful, in the view of scientific discoveries and spiritual revelation, that we stop breathing simply because we have laid our body aside—that divine process no doubt continues on some other level of existence, and our breathing is our unity with God, our Creator, as well as with our outer universe. Just as breathing is not limited to any particular race or creed, the light is also present in all (the light that enlightens every man in the world), and this realization reveals the brotherhood of mankind and the fatherhood of God. If we had the right kind of instruments, we could no doubt show that each breath is a current of light, a wave of vibrant, radiant energy . . . truly the radiation of the Almighty.

BREATHING AS A SOUND FOUNDATION

A wonderful friend of mine told a seminar on healing that we could add years of rich and vital living to our experience simply by breathing deeply ten or twelve times a day. Then he reported that the first time he tried he nearly fell on his face because his lungs just were not used to that much fresh air. Our mind, too, sometimes reels when we feed it the rich ideas of truth, but it will recover and become accustomed to the light of the world that we are.

If we are to live in the revelation of light that Jesus brought, linking it to something as permanent and practical as breathing establishes a sound foundation for growth in understanding. Start right now by entering the course of action outlined in these words: "Every time I breathe, my understanding (working knowledge) of the light of the world I am deepens and expands." Then add this reminder and instruction: "My subconscious mind acts promptly, powerfully and permanently on this course of action I have accepted consciously."

You are starting a new course of action, and you will want to have all the equipment at your disposal on the job. Repeat these statements three or four times, then be quiet until you feel your subconscious mind responding, and it will be working night and day. Your subconscious mind is the working power of the universe individualized and active in you. It is in touch with its counterpart in every other human being, and it also draws on the unlimited powers of the universal working mind. The existence and activity of this working mind is just one of the contributions of knowledge science has made to the revelation of light in recent years. Let it help you grow in understanding.

BREATHING AND THE LIGHT OF THE WORLD

You may want to expand your understanding of the link between breathing and the light of the world with ideas such as the following:

> Every time I breathe in, a current of radiant energy flows through every element of my being. Every time I breathe out, a current of radiant energy flows into my world as healing, renewing power.

Take the time to get the feel of what is happening. Do not try to force anything to happen—the light that flows in and through you does its own work.

I cannot stress too strongly the work you do in your own consciousness through meditation and the introduction of new ideas into your inner system of thought and feeling. Any miracle that takes place happens in you as greater understanding, a freer flow of radiant energy, a new insight into your own potential as the light of the world. As in all things worthwhile, you may find that it takes discipline, faith and strength to change some of the unenlightened patterns of mind and heart. It reminds me of a sign I once saw over a business firm's front entrance: "It's hard for an old rake to turn over a new leaf." It may seem difficult at first, but soon you will find that the words of Jesus have new meaning: "My yoke is easy and my burden is light."

YOUR INNER BIBLE

You are a vital part of an evolutionary program that has never stopped, and your future role in this program is up to you. The wonderful thing about this experience is that there is not a book that has been written, not even the Bible itself, that can describe what is going to happen, that can tell you exactly what your understanding is going to be, that can put into words this working knowledge. Once you have reached this point where you are ready to go directly to the light within you, you begin to draw on your own inner Bible—the "law written in your inward parts," the outer Bible phrases it. This does not mean that there is no value in books (after all, I have just written this one), and in teachings, and in religious institutions and other efforts to help humanity. It means that you must ultimately come to the point in your own individual unfoldment where you are willing to go beyond the book, beyond

the institution, beyond human opinion into a direct experience of
the light. No one else can take this path for you. No one else can
really walk it with you, and yet all the enlightened souls of eternity
walk with you when you begin your inner journey!

GIVE UP OLD CONCEPTS

Let others share their experiences with you if they are so
guided, but do not feel that your own unfoldment must duplicate
theirs. Be willing to give up old concepts, religious and otherwise,
as soon as you have grown out of them. Just as easily as light
dispels darkness in our outer world, your understanding will free
you from the misconceptions, superstitions and other limitations
of your past. You may become aware of some of the old beliefs
as the light eliminates them from your consciousness.

I remember once walking alone along a country road and
getting the message inside: "There never was such a god." As I
stopped for a few moments, I barely caught the final glimpse of
some old, unenlightened concepts of a god I had halfheartedly
entertained at the insistence of well-meaning teachers, but which
I could now release with no regret or effort. On the other hand,
your understanding of the light will eliminate many obstacles so
quietly and easily that they never reach your conscious mind at all.

THE EQUALITY OF TRUTH

If you have not been too thoroughly schooled in tradition, dogma
and ritual, the going will be easier than it is for the religious professional. In a helpful little book, *Teilhard de Chardin, A New
Synthesis of Evolution*, which bears the *nihil obstat* and *impri-
matur* of the Catholic Church, the author, Joseph V. Kopp, points
out that Teilhard de Chardin's views are difficult to swallow for
the professional theologians and sincere Christians. He says in
part: "The theologians also have difficulty in reconciling the biblical
teaching on Paradise, the Fall, and Original Sin, with the new
theories. To this is added the fear that the triumphant vision of
Christ the 'Cosmocrat,' the perfector of evolution, leaves no place
for Redemption and the Cross. Finally the biblical epiphany of
the Son is nearly eclipsed by the diaphaneity of God in the world."

He does point out that the Church cannot afford to dismiss lightly the powerful scientific forces at work in the world to discover the nature and meaning of the cosmos, and reminds readers of the unfortunate results that unenlightened attitudes toward Galileo or Darwin had for Christianity.

All I can suggest to the professional religionists of the world is that they come out from behind the sacred pulpits and rituals, the symbols and sacraments of tradition, and join the rest of humanity for a while. The truth is no respecter of persons or institutions, regardless of how formidable and sacrosanct they appear to human vision. Every revelation of truth wipes out many practices and beliefs of the past, or at least sheds new light on them.

THE UNLIMITED POWERS OF MAN

Jesus gave an answer to the dilemma when He warned against putting a new patch on an old garment and putting new wine into old wineskins. Even the "biblical" teaching on certain matters has no doubt been misinterpreted in order to get the hand of the church strengthened in times past. It is interesting to look at Paradise not as a piece of divine real estate, with gates, keys and physical dimensions, but to consider it as a potential within man. Man is obviously discovering his unlimited powers to make changes in the outer universe, and when he grows enough inside, the outer forms will come forth to produce a new earth. The "Fall" takes place every time each individual fails to live up to his *own* understanding of life or to give expression to his best, and "original sin" is no doubt man's belief in separation from his Source (God).

REDEMPTION AND THE CROSS

It seems to me that the vision of Christ the "Cosmocrat," the perfector of evolution (present in every man) leaves plenty of room for both Redemption and the Cross. The greatest job of redemption in the universe is the redemption of man's thoughts, feelings and actions from the ignorance, superstition and limitations of the past, and this requires not only the revelation and demonstration of Jesus Christ, but the continuing work of both science and enlightened religion in the present time.

The Cross gains added meaning and power when it is considered to be the demonstration of life over death, the power of light over darkness, and the freedom of the human spirit from the bondage of ignorance and fear, the "crossing out" of all belief in separation of God and man. Jesus as the demonstrator of the Christ power available to every man, and ultimately to be discovered and expressed by every man, makes sense as the Savior of mankind, the forerunner of the humanity to come, and the "light of the world." Jesus' view of God as the changeless animating Spirit behind and in all things presents a much more believable Creator than the bloodthirsty tyrant of the skies pictured by so many religious professionals. Jesus also pointed out that those who believed in Him, did not really believe in Him, but in the One who sent Him. God and man, the Father and Son are One—always have been One, always will be One, and appear to be separated only in the superstitious beliefs and concepts of man's frightened past.

UNITE YOURSELF

The power of religious concepts and tradition is immense. Even an enlightened man like Teilhard de Chardin, who was obviously plugged into the same stream of revelation that inspired Jesus, was reluctant to upset the religious applecart. If in this age of revelation, leaders in both the religious and scientific fields can join minds and hearts in the experience of growth—and there are encouraging signs on the horizon of humanity—man will at long last enter the promised land.

In any event, you need not be too concerned by what others do. You can integrate the scientist and the religionist in yourself and let your growing understanding and working knowledge of the light bring new dimensions into your experience. Praise and give thanks for your growing understanding. Take the time to appreciate your working knowledge of light. Rejoice in the progress that is taking place—after all, the Father of lights within is doing the work through His chosen instrument, YOU!

10

THE POWER TO BE: IMAGINATION

The greatest prize we can ever capture is our own imagination. In this production chamber we shape the pictures that bind or free us, heal or sicken us, prosper or impoverish us, save or condemn us. My mother was fond of telling me that each one lives in his own mind or imagination and that here is his real world, or at least the one that seems real to him. James Allen puts it this way:

> Mind is the Master-power that molds and makes,
> And Man is Mind and evermore he takes
> The Tool of Thought, and shaping what he wills,
> Brings forth a thousand joys, a thousand ills;
> He thinks in secret, and it comes to pass;
> Environment is but his looking glass.

MAN IS THE ARCHITECT

It usually comes as a shock to discover that the outer conditions of life are largely the product of our own beliefs, thoughts, feelings and above all, the images we hold of ourselves, our neighbors, life and God. To learn that conditions in body, home, human relations, bank accounts, community and even international situations are the direct result of the images held in mind by mankind is a shock—most of us probably credit life with being responsible for most of (ir difficulties. We might just be responsible for the good things that come to us, but the problems are obviously the work of some adverse power. We may even come up with a devil, a scapegoat of some kind on which to unload responsibility for our woes—or we can even blame God, who, if some of His self-styled representatives are to be believed, takes a perverse pleasure in human suffering.

But in the enlightened understanding we are entering, it is becoming more and more obvious that man is indeed the architect of his world and is responsible for the shape he and his world are in to a much greater degree than heretofore dreamed. And as some of the more enlightened observers are discerning, man is going to be almost totally responsible for the shape of the world to come. In the imagination chamber of his own being, he will lay the foundations and draw the blueprints for the world of today and tomorrow.

THE MOST POWERFUL FACTOR

The most powerful factor in the unfoldment of man (individually and as a race) is the imagination. Man is the image of God. This does not mean that God is a superman and that each man is stamped out of some cosmic dough with a divine cooky cutter shaped like the Creator. It means simply that man is the imaging end of the creative process, the individual self-expression of the unformed Divinity, the creature confronted with the responsibility of its own unfoldment, and that of the rest of the world as well, if we are willing to accept the viewpoint of scientists like Sir Alister Hardy, or the viewpoint of a spiritual leader like St. Paul, who pointed out hundreds of years ago that the whole world is in bondage and travail, waiting for the time when man comes into his own true role.

In the past, man has been the victim of his imagination because he has been ignorant of its potential and scope. The Book of Genesis says that before the Flood came that destroyed most of humanity, the hearts of men were filled with imaginations of evil of every kind, a dramatic description of what happens when the imagination of man is captured by false beliefs and fear. St. Paul of the Bible says that the human race is "in hot water" because of the type of images it holds in its mind, that the thinking of man has become futile. It has become ineffective and destructive because men have exchanged the splendor of the immortal God for an image like that of mortal man or bees or birds or outer things.

THE CREATOR AND THE CREATED

Men have forgotten the Creator and worshiped the created. They have, as Jesus pointed out, worshiped a god of form rather than the God of Truth, Spirit. The "devil" at work in the world today, as always, is the imagination of man gone awry. The present conditions in the world are an accurate outpicturing of the images man holds in his own mind, and the conditions will not permanently improve until man improves his images of the Creator, of himself, of his neighbor, of his world. When we blame outer conditions for our problems and try to cure them in outer ways only, we are like the tough old western cowboy viewing his first movie. He became so emotionally involved that he pulled out his six-shooter and shot the villain on the screen. Nothing much happened, naturally, except a few holes appeared in the screen!

THE SOURCE OF THE VILLAINY

All too often, we try to solve our problems in much the same manner. We pull out our mental, emotional and physical "guns" and try to shoot the "villain" in our lives, but nothing really happens because the source of the villainy is not "out there" on the screen. It is in the reel of pictures that is put into the projector. If we really want to change the outer picture, we must change the reel. That is the only way we can really change our lives for the better. We may try to change the screen of our lives, the outer surroundings. We may move from one section of the country to another. We may even trade wives, or husbands, or friends, or enemies, or jobs—but nothing much improves. All that happens is that we get a different screen, and sometimes a new screen shows up the glaring defects of our inner reel more clearly than the old screen. The same principle applies on the international as well as the individual scene. We can try all kinds of schemes to establish peace on the earth, but the only permanent solution is a better image in man's mind, of himself and his neighbor.

THE DAY OF JUDGMENT

If there were such a thing as a day of final judgment, the worst and first offenders to be hauled before the great judge would be those who have been responsible for the false images that infest the imagination of man. Those who have conjured up and promoted the pictures of a fierce and bloodthirsty god, a discriminatory god who favors certain races and religious groups, an eternity of condemnation, punishment and torture, man as a worthless, worm of the dust, and all the other superstitions and downright lies would no doubt be first on the divine docket—and the unhappiest verdict of all would be that they live out the images they projected.

Of course, since mankind is one and his imaginations are always projected into his experience, the day of judgment is always with us. Promoters and acceptors are alike victims of the false images, and all humanity suffers disease and death, war and concentration and torture camps, racial and religious strife, and all the "hell" that unenlightened imagination can produce. But, as a good friend of mine in Germany phrases it: "The age of viciousness is coming to an end." The old images of separation, fear, ignorance, condemnation and superstition are passing down the drain of eternity, and the age of enlightenment is finally upon us. The process of redemption, the redeeming of the subconscious or memory mind of man from the false imagery of the past is not a rapid or easy one. Old images are not like old generals—they do not just simply "fade away"—they must be done away with, or replaced with new and better ones.

EVERY MAN A WORLD LEADER

This replacement process is an individual one. We cannot depend upon leaders of religion, science, government or other areas of human endeavor to do the job for us. In a real sense, every person is a world leader. He leads a world of thought, feeling and imagination, and it is his responsibility and opportunity to capture his own imagination and redeem it, set it free to do the job it is designed to do, for his own benefit and for the benefit of all humanity. It is up to each one of us to replace the reels of limitation and superstition in his consciousness and to insert the reels of truth, light, love and life.

Never underestimate your role in the world of today and tomorrow. Often leaders in religion, government, science, business, labor and the human scene are just too busy running the "establishment" to get down to the inner discipline of changing the image pattern of humanity for the better. You can begin right now to bring "the age of viciousness" and limitation to an end in your own experience, knowing that as you improve your own images and living, a current of light and good is being made available to your fellowmen as well.

MADE IN THE IMAGE OF GOD

Why should you do this? Simply because of the way you are made. You are the image of God. Since this is true, the image you hold of yourself, of your neighbor, of your world is the image you hold or project of God, the Creator. It is your responsibility and opportunity as the imagination power of the universe individualized to hold the best possible images of all things in order that you may assume your true role as a designer and shaper of your world, and your part in the universal world of man. Your incredible role in the cosmic purpose is to image the nature of the Creator (God, Good) and bring it into self-expression by sharing it with your world. You are a divine projector, and the light of the world that you are shines through the images that you hold, projecting them onto the screen of your life, just as surely and even more accurately than the beam of light works the movie projectors of our outer world.

MAKE YOUR OWN CHOICE

My delightful friend, Dr. Maxwell Maltz, one of the world's outstanding plastic surgeons, and author of the splendid book *Psycho-Cybernetics* emphasizes again and again the importance of improving our self-image if we really intend to make any substantial improvement in our contribution to the world in which we live. Even "positive" thinking and prayer are ineffective if we insist on hanging on to inadequate self-images. The imagination wins out, but the wonderful thing is that we can make changes in the images we hold of ourselves and others quite readily. It is mostly a matter of conscious choice—at least initially. And we do have a wide range, indeed, to choose from. If we consider the religious field, we find we can choose (and probably have chosen) an image all the way from a worthless sinner, luckless worm of the dust, on up the scale to the image of God, a child of God, a life-giving Spirit, the light of the world. In the scientific field we might choose the image of a biological freak, a chemical accident, a few dollars' worth of chemicals and minerals, a hundred-plus pounds of flesh and blood, the top creature in a chain of evolutionary processes, the self-expression of a creative activity, and again the light of the world.

Society has some unique images of its own—the images of failure or success, a member of an "inferior" or "superior" race or religion, conformist or nonconformist group, "In" or "Out" political or social group, a "rugged" individualist or a cowering "Milquetoast," "black" power, "white" power, "money" power, "poverty" power—all these and countless other images are available to the individual, and it is up to the individual to make his own choice—but, of course, he is stuck in the image of his choice until he decides to exchange it for a better one.

A STEP IN THE RIGHT DIRECTION

Every improvement in our self-image is a step in the right direction, a movement away from the facelessness and self-suppression favored by so many in this day of pressure on true selfhood. Only you can decide if you have had enough of old images, inner pictures of limitation, and that you are ready to step forward in the light of your own divine self-image. If you are in agreement, take the step toward a better self-image now. Capture your own imagination, free it from the reel of limited images that have hampered its operation, and set it to work on its true assignment, picturing your potential as the light of the world!

THE MAGIC WAND

Dr. Donald Hatch Andrews gives an imaginative picture of the "unseen" and the "unheard" world of which we are the self-expression:

> If I could wave a magic wand before you and give you the power to perceive all the invisible sights and inaudible sounds around you at this moment, what would you see and what would you hear?
>
> Close your eyes for a moment. I wave the wand. Now look about you. The room is ablaze with dazzling light. The chairs, the tables, the floor, the ceiling, and the walls are prismatic crystals, sparkling with a thousand shades of red, yellow, green, and blue such as you have never in your life seen before. Your clothes are on fire with a million microscopic rainbow flames. Your nose, your cheeks, your hands are shining ruby, emerald, and sapphire. You open your mouth and a shaft of amethyst light beams out before you. The air itself sparkles as if millions of miniature meteors are darting all around you, as if a cluster of skyrockets had just exploded. There is a swift rain of tiny incandescent bullets shooting down from the ceiling, shooting through the table, through the chairs, right through your body and disappearing into the floor.
>
> Almost blinded by this strange blaze of light, you shut your eyes in bewilderment. I now press the magic wand on your ears. Suddenly you are aware of a hurricane of sound beating upon you, as if a thousand symphony orchestras were magically squeezed into the room and all playing fortissimo. For every object near you is resonating with its own strange, peculiar music. The table booms like a hundred big bass fiddles doing a bolero. The lamp is trilling like a dozen flutes. The carpet is caroling. In this very book you hold in your hand, you hear a chorus of a thousand voices. And your body is vibrant with the most complex music of all. . . .

THE INVISIBLE KINGDOM

Dr. Andrews points out that the latest scientific discoveries reveal that the nature of the universe is not matter, but light and music. In speaking of the invisible kingdom, he states:

> This is the realm of the unseen and the unheard that shines and pulsates around you and within you unperceived during every moment of your life. But though invisible and inaudible, it is just as real as everything that you actually see and hear and feel. It is the domain in which scientists are beginning to discover more and more of the

secrets of life and of the universe. For this unseen and unheard is not science fiction. In scientific laboratories all over the world thousands of experiments have been performed that establish the reality of these unperceived phenomena beyond any shadow of doubt, that prove that these waves of unseen "light" and unheard "sound" are truly around us and within us at all times.

In the "light" religion and science meet. In the "light" and through the "light" the God (or Creator) of both religion and science moves to bring forth the universe and reveal the mystery of the divine nature. From the "light" both religion and science will draw the inspiration and energy to move ahead together in the next great stage of human unfoldment. Each person is a self-conscious expression of the "light" and he has access to its great mysteries not only through the research programs of laboratories, but directly through the expansion of his own faith, his own awareness, his own understanding, his own experience, his own imagination, his own willingness to become its image.

THE DIVINE POTENTIAL

Perhaps the "hereafter" man has always instinctively sought is right *here*, *after* he awakens to what is in and around him, available for self-expression through him. Moses was not exaggerating when he said that man is the image of God; Jesus was accurate when He taught that "the kingdom of God" is within man; Paul hit the target when he declared that man ultimately becomes a "life-giving spirit." Not only is this invisible realm "not science fiction," it is not religious fiction either. It is real, alive, vibrant—available to the one whose imagination permits him to enter it and it to enter him.

Just as science is discovering the nature of the universe in the light that authors and sustains it, so will each individual discover the nature of his own divine potential as he probes into and becomes the light of the world that he is. There is one light, and in that radiant energy is the nature of the Creator, the substance out of which the spiritual, mental, emotional, physical universe and all the creatures in it are made. The light is the divine stuff out of which all the elements of the God Man of the future are to be drawn by each individual as he awakens to his own possibilities and the adventure in living that lies ahead.

THE NATURE OF GOD

There are many wonderful books that are designed and written to help people improve their status in life. They contain good ideas for increasing income, improving human relations, establishing peace of mind and healing a thousand human ills and lacks. These are all fine. Anything that helps man overcome his ignorance, poverty and sickness in any area of life is a blessing and part of the enlightenment of human consciousness. Every step upward from the bog of human bondage is a movement of the light toward greater light, acting through the imagination of man, preparing him for acceptance of the image of God that he is. This book is concerned with man, or to be more specific, you, as the image of God. You are designed to be the image of God, a self-expression of the Infinite, the light of the world!

Someone long ago observed that in the beginning God made man in His image, and man has been returning the compliment ever since. It is finally dawning on men that the nature of God is much more like light, energy, spirit, music, love, faith than a superman figure in some distant sky, parceling out life on a distinctly "human" basis. Your image of God, your image of light, includes all the other images you will ever need. Jesus pointed out that when we seek the "kingdom of God and its righteousness" (light), all the other things we need for existence in this earth experience will "be added."

THE RICHEST EXPERIENCE

As you stir up your imagination to accept the image of light, you need not be concerned that you are on your way to poverty row—you are in for the richest living experiences you have ever had. As you improve your self-image, the light systems of your body will be electrified, your human relations will sparkle with interest and vitality, your work or business will throb with new life, and your mental and emotional energy fields will be stimulated to new heights of performance. You will be living in the light!

Remember that while it takes imagination to enter and experience this field or ocean of light, it is not an imaginary thing at all. As your imagination strengthens through exercise, the light will become the most real part of your make-up. Even though the words you use initially may seem to be merely words, keep on until the activity they describe becomes rich and meaningful to you. This field of light is so great that you can never exhaust its energy, and the highest image you can conceive is easily within the range of its power of fulfillment. Remind yourself that you are the imaging or imaginative end of this process of light and exercise your part in the creative action of the universe with a growing confidence.

AN IMAGINATION EXERCISE

Now, for an exercise in imagination, begin with the understanding you presently have of the great truth that you are the image of God! As the image of God, it is your privilege and responsibility to picture the good you are willing to have expressed in and through you. As a matter of disconcerting fact, you cannot evade this privilege and responsibility. Your imagination is always producing pictures (even a blank is a picture of nothing), and the radiant energy of the universe, the light of the world, is always projecting these pictures into your living experience.

For a foundation, consider the truth in the following words: *I AM the image of God, the self-expression of the light of the world.* Repeat this idea a few times, meditating on it in the light of some of the ideas that your mind has gleaned from earlier chapters of this book. Your own prayer periods and drills in the light will bear rich fruit now. Then, for a little personal practice, complete the following statement in your own way: *As the light of the world, I have a _____ picture of myself.* Select your adjectives as they come to your conscious mind and consider them a bit before you pass them along to your subconscious mind for filing in your memory cabinet. In capturing your imagination and disciplining it, you are exercising the power that can lift man to the skies of achievement and fulfillment—or keep him in the grinding ruts of bondage and frustration when it is left unguarded and ungoverned.

THE IMAGES THAT GOVERN

You cannot make, or permit, a single picture that is not out-pictured to some degree in your outer life, because that "light of the world that you are" shines straight through the image that you, its self-expression, hold. The images that you hold in your imagination chamber govern your life with a precision that is beyond calculation.

In his practice as a plastic surgeon, Dr. Maxwell Maltz discovered to his amazement that some of his patients who had undergone a "successful" surgical operation remained as unhappy as before because they would not or could not release their mental and emotional scars from the inner images or pictures they carried of themselves, and others. Doctors, counselors and ministers are often appalled by the waste of talent in those who come for help and are incapable of using their real abilities because of the inferior images they hold of themselves. And often it seems easier to transplant an organ in the physical body than it is to replace a poor image in the imagination chamber. But it can be done.

A successful man told me that his early life was a struggle, not because he did not have opportunities and the ability to take advantage of them, but his own self-image made him afraid to move ahead. He said that when he first started school, he could barely speak English because another language was spoken at home. In fact, he was so shy the first day at school that he wet his pants rather than dare to ask where the toilets were. For a long time, he carried a self-image of a "dumb, fearful, inadequate foreigner" in his mind—but one day the "light" dawned in him, and he realized he was not that limited self at all. He said that his improving self-image brought an improvement in his fortunes and the feeling of being able to assume a greater role in life. "I feel," he summarized, "that the greatest contribution education can make to anyone is to teach him how to hold an adequate self-image of himself and his family."

THE USE OF IMAGINATION

Now that we are discovering something of the potential of our imagination, let's use it confidently and creatively. A Nigerian philosopher friend of mine (he is a cook and does his philosophizing on the side) made this sage observation: "I don't understand so-called religious people. They pray, but they don't use their heads. If they used their heads, they wouldn't have to pray so much!"

When we use our imagination constructively and consciously, we will find that we do not have to pray so much—or probably more accurately, the nature of our prayer changes completely, from begging or whining to praise and thanksgiving.

EXPAND YOUR IMAGINATION

Here are a few ideas for expanding your own exercise in imagination, but change the words to suit your own understanding and feeling.

As the light of the world, I have a healthy, prosperous, happy picture of myself.

Or, in the light of the ideas we are pursuing:

As the light of the world, I have a confident, willing, understanding, imaginative, enthusiastic, convincing picture of myself.

As the light of the world, I have a loving, wise, joyous, strong, growing, lively picture of myself.

As the light of the world, I have an enlightened, delightful picture of myself.

Be willing to experiment, to move into new and uncharted courses of action. All the progress in the world of man has come about because someone had the courage to get a new picture of himself, his world, his contribution to society. "Without vision [imagination], the people perish," the Bible puts it, and now is the time to stop wasting energy supporting images that make us sick, unhappy, inefficient, fearful—early candidates for the undertaker's skill.

YOUR WONDERFUL POWER

Your own experience is the best guide for you to follow in directing your wonderful power of imagination. Some of the new pictures of yourself may seem startling and beyond reach at first, but the reminder that you are in reality the image of God, the imaging end of the creative process, will help you realize how unlimited your capacity to achieve is. You need not be too concerned with specific courses of action, jobs, amounts of money, and the like. The Old Testament warns against making "graven," or rigid and limited images of God. Your imagination is a conversion chamber that takes ideas like light, love, faith, life and converts them into patterns and form. Words, themselves, are images in verbal form and are helpful in our working with the power of imagination. Turning your imagination loose on the word "light" is opening your whole life to new experiences.

For practice, you may wish to visualize or image the light filling your mind completely, erasing unenlightened patterns and habits of thought, and replacing them with images of light, achievement, joy, strength and vitality. You will soon discover that your imagination becomes the instrument of light, which is as it should be because "you are the light of the world," and imagination is one of your powers to be.

Then you can move into your emotional nature by imaging the light flowing into it, dissolving unenlightened feelings of resentment, fear or burden, and releasing the emotions of light, joy, love and gratitude. Once again, you will soon discover that your emotional nature, or heart, is the instrument of the light of the world that you are, designed to give expression to that light.

HEALING AND RENEWAL

If you are the fortunate operator of a vivid and flexible imagination, you will receive healing and renewal from this exercise:

Find a comfortable position, mentally, emotionally and physically and remind yourself that your body is a temple of the living God (the light of the world) then see or image the light filling your physical body. Watch it flow through your brain, into your nervous system, moving throughout your body turning on the light in every atom, cell and organ. Feel the light rejuvenate and revitalize the electrical systems of your body; rejoice as it eliminates the short circuits and knots that false images have imposed on your biological and chemical units. Watch the light flow into your physical heart and bloodstream, purifying and strengthening them until your whole body is washed in a current of light.

No doubt this is what actually happens all the time, in accordance with our faith and understanding. Perhaps the seemingly cannibalistic statement of Jesus that His followers had to eat his flesh and drink his blood are understandable in the light of our scientific discoveries of the true nature of the universe! Light or radiant energy is the substance of all form, including flesh and blood.

GIVE THINGS THE LIGHT TOUCH

The image contained in the following words may give you a lift: "I rejoice in the light as it streamlines, slenderizes, tunes up and energizes my body." This is not a somber, heavy-minded exercise— let it be a lighthearted experience. After all, your body is the residence (mental, emotional, physical) of the light of the world that you are, and its rooms, functions and organs of operation respond to the truth. A lovely friend of ours, whose vitality, beauty and resilience thrill all who meet her, responds when asked her secret: "I have learned to give things the light touch." The touch of light—how eager our overburdened, darkened minds, hearts and bodies are to respond to the words, the thoughts, the feelings, the images of light! Just to check up on yourself, take a quick peek into a mirror right after you have practiced the Drill in the Light.

Now take an imaginative look at the fields of living energy in which your body lives and moves. See the light flowing into these force fields of energy, rejuvenating them constantly and raising their vibration level closer and closer to the wave lengths of light itself. More and more you will be able to catch the true image of yourself as the self-expression of light, and you and your world will be delighted at the new freedom and radiance you express.

EXTEND YOUR IMAGINATION

Naturally, you will extend the power of your imagination for the benefit of others and begin to release them from any reels of limitation you may hold concerning them. You are to love your neighbor as yourself, and one of the best and most effective ways to love your neighbor is to get the right image of him. The images we hold of each other are powerful influences on our behavior and reactions. The same principles and courses of action you are finding so effective with yourself will work in the inventory of pictures you hold of others. You cannot help but have an image of everyone in your life—so make it a good one! To behold him as the light of the world is a good start now that you have the religious and scientific justification for this picture.

You are the light of the world. It is your responsibility and privilege to bring light to every part and activity of that world. You have the opportunity to hold the best possible image of every situation and activity that includes you. Your work, your home, your community, your friendships, your problems—all these are excellent candidates for an exercise in imagination and will benefit from a new picture. The world of wholeness, abundance, peace and joy is not a figment of the imagination—it is real, vibrant, already present within us as the light of the world waiting to come into expression through the images we permit it to form in us.

Much more can be written about imagination. It is an inexhaustible power. Tap its infinite resources, beginning right now, and live imaginatively and creatively.

11

THE POWER TO BE:
ENTHUSIASM

There is no room in the heaven of rich and successful living for the lukewarm. ". . . You are neither cold nor hot. . . . So, because you are lukewarm, and neither cold nor hot, I will spit you out of my mouth." (Rev. 3:16 NEB) Life drops us by the wayside unless we accept its treasures wholeheartedly. There is little reward in a lukewarm approach to the Light. Enthusiasm is a wonderful quality of light. It is the energy that sparks or ignites our other powers. To be enthusiastic is to be possessed by or literally "on fire" with God. In our enthusiasm, the light of the world that we are becomes a living flame that consumes doubt, fear, procrastination and hesitancy. Enthusiasm "fires" us into a new orbit of mental, emotional and physical performance. Enthusiasm is the sparkplug of our being. Enthusiasm is the ignition coil of life, and without it we are dead spiritually.

THE IMPORTANCE OF INNER CONVERSION

Unfortunately much of the religious fervor, zeal and enthusiasm have gone into attempts to convert humanity to some particular form of religious belief and practice, rather than into the more important work of inner conversion on the part of each individual.

Jesus' instruction to go into the world and preach the gospel has largely been interpreted as an outer missionary effort to herd the heathen into some denominational camp. The deeper meaning of preaching the gospel to the heathen images in our own conscious-ness has often been overlooked and neglected, to the detriment of both the individual and true religion.

It has been pointed out that religion would be easier to accept if it were not for the so-called "religionists"—the zealots who preach but do not practice. To paraphrase Emerson: What they are has made such a racket, it has been hard to believe what they said. Or as my dad, who was an astute observer of the human religious scene, said to an overardent, would-be evangelist who visited us and told us in booming tones of the way to salvation and what a hot reception we would have in the beyond if we did not follow his instructions implicitly: "Someone could disagree with you and not necessarily be wrong. If there is such a thing as a place called heaven—and if you get there, you'll be pretty upset by those who are there, and probably even more amazed by those who don't make it. If you used your energy on and in yourself, you wouldn't have to preach so loud and long."

THE BEST MISSIONARY

I realize that there are many wonderful people in organized religion who have been an inspiration and help to many as they have been to me—but the missionary thrust has often been a mis-directed one. We are witnessing the spectacle now of many coun-tries closing the doors to missionaries of denominational bias and even throwing them out if they are too violent in their approach. I talked with an official of an African government who told me that while the churches had done fine work in establishing and operating hospitals and schools, the net result had been deep divi-sions religiously in the population, and that this type of religion could not long be tolerated by people who believed in the unity of humanity. In a mission school, I talked with the headmaster who told me that while he was teaching in a religious organization, he knew nothing about God, and that it was a revelation to him to learn that the kingdom of God was within, not a paradise in the sky.

The best missionary in the world is not one who hurls words and threats at reluctant human beings, but a person who is on fire with the light of the world and who recognizes its presence and power in all he contacts in any way. Words are fine only when they are the overflow of an enthusiastic, enlightened mind and heart.

THE TROUBLE WITH CONCEPTS OF HEAVEN . . .

Individuals close their minds to the fearful, lackluster, anemic pictures that have been presented of "heaven." It is difficult to generate much enthusiasm for some of the concepts and dogmas that have come down from supposed authorities. I recall from my boyhood experiences the time a chum came wailing up to me and reported that he had just received a thrashing from his mother. I asked why, and he said: "Because I told her I didn't want to go to heaven." Since I was already developing some inner reservations on this subject myself, I kept digging: "What did you tell her?" He blurted out: "I told her I didn't want to go to heaven because I was afraid that it would be just like Sunday school and church and probably the same kind of people would be in charge—and I just couldn't see putting up with that forever!"

The spirit of independence and truth in each one can put up with only so much "hogwash" before it rebels, and more and more thinking persons are moving mentally, emotionally and physically out of the reach of traditional religious concepts. In this age of individual unfoldment, many are realizing the truth that religion starts as an inside job, an inner worship that develops a personality that becomes a light in the world—a light that those who see can accept as a potential of their own being also.

THE MOST ENTHUSIASTIC MAN

Notwithstanding some of the colorless, unhappy pictures presented of Jesus, He must have been the most enthusiastic man in history. When one begins to realize that the teaching of Jesus promised more life, more love and more joy to those who accept it, one can begin to share that enthusiasm and zeal. He not only glowed with enthusiasm about that "kingdom" within Himself, He joyously reported its presence and power within all humanity, enough to fire the enthusiasm of us all! He said: "The kingdom of heaven is like a treasure lying buried in a field. The man found it, buried it again; and for sheer joy went and sold everything he had, and bought that field" (Matt. 13:44), and again: "Here is another picture of the kingdom of Heaven. A merchant looking out for fine pearls found one of a very special value; so he went and sold everything he had, and bought it." (Matt. 13:45, 46)

THE INNER TREASURE

In these glowing illustrations, we can sense the enthusiasm of the persons involved. And, of course, when we pass from the superficial implications sufficiently to realize that the treasure and the pearl symbolize the inner light or kingdom of God within, we are soon on the way to a new enthusiasm for living. We are willing to sell everything we have, or to give up all our past concepts in order to lay hold of the new revelation wholeheartedly. When we find this treasure, we bury it again. We recognize that we are faced with an "inside job." We have an inner work to do. The "light" is more than a subject of conversation. It is more than a religious concept to foist off on the world. It is an inner treasure to be brought into radiant expression through the exercise of faith, will, understanding, imagination and now—ENTHUSIASM!

"STIR INTO FLAME . . ."

Paul, another enthusiastic advocate of the inner light or spirit, wrote to his friend Timothy: "That is why I now remind you to stir into flame the gift of God which is within you . . . for the spirit that God gave us is no craven spirit, but one to inspire strength, love and self-discipline." (II Tim. 1:6, 7)

Here again we have a picture of an "inside job," the acceptance and stirring into action of an inner light or spirit that has been buried for generations and centuries in the darkness of human ignorance and superstition. This light shines constantly, but we benefit from its power only as we grasp it and make it part of our own being. The process by which we lay hold of the light and stir it up finds outer application in our atom-smashing equipment. In the "atom-smashers" a beam of light is caught up by magnets and accelerated until it flows at such a terrific rate that it can strike a substance and break off electrons and atoms releasing tremendous amounts of energy. In us, the light beam (the light of the world we are) is caught up and accelerated by the magnetic centers of faith, will, understanding, imagination, enthusiasm, love and others until it releases unsuspected energies and talents in our own being. If your imagination is active enough, you will easily get the picture of the process within yourself, and the picture will help to stir the light into a living flame.

SELL YOURSELF FIRST

One of the most enthusiastic, and best, salesmen I have ever known told me how he stirred up his enthusiasm for a new product before he ever went into a customer's place of business to try to sell it. He said he took the time to look over the product carefully, study the manufacturer's selling points, test the product in any way possible, visualize how he or others could use it, the benefits it would bring the user—in short, he "sold" himself on the new product, and when his enthusiasm was flowing, selling his customers was almost incidental. He refused to sell an inferior product, and his customers soon learned and appreciated that fact. He sold great quantities of merchandise because he was "on fire" with his products.

As the light of the world, we are concerned with an enterprise much more rewarding than any commercial activity, wonderful and rich though that may be. The "light of the world" is by far the richest, finest product in the universe, and it should be easy to sell ourselves on it.

PRAISE AND THANKSGIVING

A brief analysis of the procedure used by my salesman friend to stir up his enthusiasm reveals that he actually used the process of praise and thanksgiving prescribed in the Bible. To praise is to see, acknowledge, discover the presence of good in anything, and to give thanks is to magnify, increase, appreciate the value of that good in ourselves through the exercise of gratitude. Praise and thanksgiving (appreciation) always lead to a state of enthusiasm. To praise and appreciate the light is to surrender enthusiastically and wholeheartedly to it—to become possessed by it, to be aglow with it.

EXERCISES IN ENTHUSIASM

Following are exercises, or courses of action, described in words to stir up your enthusiasm for the light. The words are verbal images or symbols of the action they describe and are meant to be used only as guides. Get into the activity they describe as quickly as possible. A word of instruction to your responsive working or subconscious mind will help. You might phrase it this way:

"I am enthusiastic about the way my subconscious mind carries out the actions described in the words I speak or think" or

"I praise and appreciate my subconscious mind as it translates my words into the actions they describe."

Again, I remind you that you are your own formula for success in anything you undertake—use these words if they are meaningful to you. If you have more effective ones, use them. The important thing is to get under way on stirring up your enthusiasm.

Now for further exercise in enthusiasm, consider the actions in the following words:

I stir up my enthusiasm through the practice of praise and appreciation.

I praise and appreciate the light of the world that I am.

Now move deeper into the exercise. Think about the good things you already know about the light:

Light is the radiant energy out of which all things are made.

Light is the inexhaustible field of living energy in which your mental, emotional, physical body exists.

Light is the activity of God, the radiation of the Divine Nature.

Light clears your mind, lifts your emotions and rejuvenates your body.

Go beyond words—praise and appreciate the light of the world you are. Even a little practice will deepen and expand your understanding of praise and appreciation, and you will feel your enthusiasm warming up. Keep on—sell yourself on the light.

You may wish to expand the exercise in other ways. For example: "I am enthusiastic and utterly delighted about the marvelous way the light clears my mind, purifies my emotions and energizes my body" or, "I am enthusiastic about the light that fills my mind with rich ideas and gives me the energy to carry them out."

APPROACH THE THRONE WITH BOLDNESS

In your exercise of enthusiasm, let yourself go. For short periods, at least, depart from conventional habits of thought and imagination. You are no "craven spirit" or unworthy, lackluster, downtrodden worm of the dust. You are the image of God, the light of the world. Approach the throne of grace with boldness. Be audacious in your handling of the light. Ask, affirm, proclaim, believing that that radiant cosmic energy available for self-expression through you is capable of fulfilling the finest image you can hold in overflowing measure. Stir the light of the world in you into a living flame that warms and energizes all the elements of your being and galvanizes you into inspired action.

THE ELUSIVE FORMULA

You will have noticed that this book is designed to plug you into the activity of stirring up the powers of your own being. All too often we merely read books about the truth or light; we may go to lectures about wonderful subjects and return to our world temporarily uplifted—but if we really mean business, we ultimately find ourselves exercising the "self-discipline" Paul urged on his friend Timothy.

For centuries, humanity has largely sought a magic formula, an instant savior, a miraculous religion to save it from bondage. We often generate much enthusiasm about religious, mental, and even physical diets until we discover that to reap the benefits they offer we have to follow them—and then rather than pay the price demanded (sell everything we have), we go drifting along with the mob. We may run from church to church, religion to religion, savior to savior, person to person, doctor to doctor, looking for that "magic something" that will be our salvation. How we would all love to ride into "heaven" on someone else's coattails. We find, however, that when we catch up with a real savior, or he catches up with us, he always points to our own inner potential as the way out of bondage into freedom.

The "light," the kingdom of good we seek, is always within us, and that is why I urge you to become involved in your own un-foldment, the activity that frees you to be what you are. It is my desire that long before you finish reading this book, you will be so completely caught up in new courses of spiritual, mental, emotional and physical actions that your friends will be delighted, and even your enemies (if you have any) will be inspired.

For too long, humanity has been so burdened by false images of restriction and violence that it takes consistent self-discipline enthusiastically applied to free the individual from the collective load of falsity and superstition. You can help yourself immensely by entering into the action described in the following words: "I am enthusiastic about the wonderful way my whole being enters into the activity described in the words I read."

THE "MAGIC SOMETHING"

There is a "magic something" that does indeed lead to salvation, freedom from our self-accepted or self-imposed limitations. Jesus spoke of it when He said: "I am the way and the truth and the life . . . I am the resurrection and the life . . . No one comes to the Father except by me." And, of course, He referred to it again when He pointed out, "You are the light of the world."

In each instance, the "I am," the "me," the "You are," is the "magic something," the individual potential, the light of the world awaiting recognition, acceptance and expression through everyone. Jesus even pointed out that the time would come when it would no longer be necessary for Him to pray or intercede for His followers because they would be directly plugged into the divine source. You are the way the truth comes to life in your world—the Christ or reality within you is your resurrection and life—and you can come to the Father only through the expansion and development of your own selfhood.

TOWARD A NEW EXPERIENCE

Now, let's stir up your enthusiasm for this "magic something" that you are. Here's a course of action described in words that can lead you into a new experience if you are willing to follow it that far:

I am enthusiastic about the self-expression of the Infinite that I am.

I am enthusiastic about my growing ability to recognize, accept and express my real potential.

I am enthusiastic about my growing confidence (faith) in the light of the world that I am.

I am enthusiastic about my growing willingness to individualize the will of God in all that concerns me.

I am enthusiastic about my growing understanding, working knowledge, of the light of the world.

I am enthusiastic about my growing ability to image the good available for expression through me.

I am enthusiastic about my growing delight in the radiant energy that flows into self-expression through and as me.

I praise and give thanks (to the Father of lights) for the way, the truth and the life that I am.

I am enthusiastic about the unsuspected powers of self-expression that are coming to light in my consciousness.

I am enthusiastic about the new mental, emotional and physical activity that the light inspires in me.

I am enthusiastic about the light, the radiant energy, the living flame that consumes every vestige of false belief, every negative pattern of thought and feeling.

I am enthusiastic about the light of the world that is becoming a personal living experience for me.

Whenever a statement "pulls a trigger" in you, if "it rings a bell" of recognition and delight, stop reading and meditate on it. The important thing is not that you finish reading a certain number of words, but that you respond to an idea that changes the mental action that transforms your living habits for the better. We are creatures of habit, and every time we start a new, constructive habit we are new creatures. Become enthusiastic about your growing ability to let old images and the habits they generate slip away.

DEVELOP SELF-ENTHUSIASM

You are getting a new picture of yourself as a creature of light. Put your enthusiasm into it! Declare to your inner system of thought and feeling: "I am enthusiastic about myself as a being of light. I am utterly delighted by the pearl of great price, the light of the world that I am."

Get an enthusiastic picture of your mind as the mind of light, of your heart as a circulator of light, of your body as a temple of light. Think enthusiastically of your body as more than flesh and blood. Image it as a body of light, radiant energy. Picture the living fields of force or energy in which the so-called physical elements of your body are embedded, the ocean of light and music surrounding you, from which you draw vitality and strength with every breath. In fact, you might put some enthusiasm into your breathing through the course of action in these words: "I am enthusiastic about the breath of the Almighty as it pumps radiant energy through my whole being." Be enthusiastic about this shining breath, rejoice in it, give thanks for it, praise it.

While enthusiasm has its origin in heaven, it finds expression in the activities of earth—so let even the cells of your body in on your enthusiasm. Each cell is an intelligent, responsive unit of light. Rutherford Platt, in an article in *Reader's Digest* magazine, points out that "scientists are learning that the miniature world of the single living cell is as astonishing as man himself." Each cell is a universe in itself and an integral part of your total being. Others have already pointed out that each person has the greatest listening audience in the universe—the cells, organs and functions of his own body—and that the whole outer universe is but an extension of man's body. Your enthusiasm is catching—let the cells of your body catch fire from your inner enthusiastic acceptance of the light of the world and the energy that operates them. You might say: "I am enthusiastic about the refreshing way the cells of my body accept and use the light of the world I am" or, "I am delighted by the energy that fills my body with light and music and lifts my whole being to the vibration level of health and strength."

Hook your imagination and enthusiasm together and lift your expectation level. Link your faith, will, understanding, imagination and enthusiasm into a magnificent instrument of self-expression through which the light of the world shines to benefit the whole world.

TAKE A NEW LOOK

Take a new look at your work, home, human relations, friendships and other activities in your life. Get a new picture of each one as an avenue through which the light shines. Think of each contact with another human being as an opportunity to express more and more of your own self-potential as the light of the world. Let your light shine so enthusiastically and wholeheartedly and effortlessly that all who see it will recognize its presence and potential within themselves! Your own inner enthusiasm for the light of the world in you and others will put a twinkle in your mind, a glow in your heart and a sparkle in your eyes and face. Enthusiasm is contagious, and when it is genuine, everyone in your world will respond to it. If you are a father or mother of a family, its members will soon be wondering: "I wonder what's happening to dad (or mom). There's a new light in his (or her) eyes—a new zest for living. I'm glad he (or she) has eased up on the lecturing and become a real human being for a change. It's fun to be around him (or her)." You'll find that you speak less often, but more meaningfully, and more effectively, and you will soon develop much enthusiasm for the potential of each member of your family.

If you happen to be a clergyman and your enthusiasm for the inner light, both in yourself and the members of your congregation, is genuine, you may begin overhearing remarks like these: "The 'parson' is getting a new lease on life. The light's really turned on in him." "By golly, I really believe he believes what he's saying. He's on fire with it." "I'm glad he stopped belting us over the head with our sins and is letting us know what's right with us for a change. I'm well enough acquainted with my shortcomings, but I'm glad to find some help in improving myself." "It's getting easier to believe what he says because of what he's becoming." "It's great to discover that there's some hope for humanity and that each one can take part in a new world."

If you're the head of a business, a genuine enthusiasm for the light potential of yourself and your employees and customers can work miracles. You may hear comments like these, either inadvertently or because someone enthusiastically reports them to you: "Boy, the boss is really turned on. He believes in himself and I think he believes in me, too." "I like the twinkle in the 'old man's' eye and the easy, relaxed way he has of doing business." "I drive with my gas gauge on empty for miles just to buy gas at that fellow's service station. It gives me a lift just to drive in." "I like to work for him. His enthusiasm for life and the potential of others turns me on, too."

If you happen to be a teacher of our boys and girls, your enthusiasm for the light in you and in them will send a glow into generations to come. Our young people respond to enthusiasm, and the light in them becomes a living flame when we recognize it and praise and appreciate it into greater expression. Long after I had forgotten much of the instruction I had received from a professor in psychology, I remembered his enthusiasm for life and his comment that success came to those who stirred up their "enthusi-oozee-asm." As he put it, "enthusi-oozee-asm has'm."

FIRE THE SPARKPLUG

No matter what your work or position in life is, fire the sparkplug of your enthusiasm. Let it energize and stir into action all the elements of your being. Let it lay hold of the light of the world you are and fan it into a living flame that brings joy and inspiration into the experience of everyone whose life you enter. Remember that you are no "craven spirit," locked into a world of limitation. You are the light of the world. Begin right now to think, feel, speak and act like it.

12

THE POWER TO BE:
AUTHORITY

Around the turn of the century, an open-souled poet, Edwin Markham, after seeing Millet's world-famous painting, "The Man with the Hoe," asked these penetrating questions:

> Who made him dead to rapture and despair.
> . . . Whose breath blew out the light within this brain?
> Is this the Thing the Lord God made and gave
> To have dominion over sea and land,
> To trace the stars and search the heavens for power,
> To feel the passion of Eternity?
>   . . .
>
> O masters, lords and rulers in all lands,
> Is this the handiwork you give to God,
> This monstrous thing distorted and soul-quenched?
> How will you ever straighten up this shape,
> Touch it again with immortality;
> Give back the upward looking and the light;
> Rebuild in it the music and the dream;
> Make right the immemorial infamies,
> Perfidious wrongs, immedicable woes?
> O masters, lords and rulers in all lands,
> How will the Future reckon with this Man?
> How answer his brute question in that hour

When whirlwinds of rebellion shake the world?
How will it be with kingdoms and with kings—
With those who shaped him to the things he is—
When this dumb Terror shall reply to God,
After the silence of the centuries?

THE MAN SPIRIT WITHIN US

The silence of the centuries is being broken by the spirit of man, and the whirlwinds of rebellion are shaking the world. The Man is no longer just the "man with the hoe." He is now also the man in the ghetto—the man in Harlem—the man in Berkeley, Yale, Columbia, Harvard, Paris, Moscow, Peking—the man in the plush penthouse on Fifth Avenue, in the cracker boxes of Facelessville, Suburbia, in the roboted acres of the industrial plant—the man in the Beatnik role, the Hippie costume, the draft card burner pose.

In short, the "man with the hoe" is the Man Spirit within all of us. It is stirring into wakefulness after centuries of fits and starts, after generations of suppression, distortion, exploitation, ignorance and superstition. "Who shaped him to the thing he is?" All humanity has had a hand in this shaping, and all humanity suffers the pain of this misshaping, this distortion of the light of the world that man is, this warping of the human potential. Almost without exception, the instruments of organized society—religion, science, business, education, labor, tradition, habit—have conspired to delay man's coming into his own. Each segment has come up with its own image of man, its own tight little formulas of human good, and then worked to shape man in these images. Religion's image of man as a "worm of the dust," science's view of man as a few cents' worth of chemicals, business' and labor's concept of man as a cog in the machine of commerce, education's attempts to pour light into a supposedly ignorant brain—all the images of conformity and limitation that have been poured into the imagination chamber of man are contributors to the "shape" he is expressing and experiencing. All the attempts to make man a "ward" of any organization, or for that matter, even of God, are doomed to failure because of what man is, the self-expression of the Infinite, the Light of the World.

WHEN MAN MOVES IN REBELLION

"How will it be with kingdoms and with kings—with those who shaped him to the thing he is"—when man moves in rebellion? They are in for a rough time—a time of reappraisal, revision, growth, change, probably even obliteration. When the evolution of the Spirit of Man is too long delayed by ignorance, superstition, tradition, greed, inertia and other forms of unenlightenment, it explodes into revolution and rebellion. The Man Spirit becomes fed up with the false images it has been given (or perhaps, even more accurately, it has given itself) and strikes out in frustration, desperation, anger and violence at its seeming enemies—the organizations, individuals (kingdoms and kings) that block its way to greater self-expression. Perhaps the whole universe quakes as the god that is to govern in the ages ahead blindly and violently flexes its muscles and tears apart the civilization it has erected in response to the images it has carried of itself.

The spirit of rebellion may seem to center in the youth of the day—those who have not yet been integrated comfortably, complacently, profitably or hopelessly into the "establishment," the ruling kingdoms of the human scene. It usually has taken the instruments of society some twenty or more years to blow out the light of individuality and to impress the stamp of conformity on its children, although there are, fortunately, some sturdy individuals who never succumb completely to organized mediocrity. In any event, the Man Spirit is active in varying degrees in people of all age groups, and rebellion, active and potential, threatens every area of human experience.

Man is being reborn, a new awareness and understanding is entering his consciousness, a new image of himself—his needs, desires and potential—is slowly taking shape. Like a chick in the egg, man's first effort in the new direction of evolution is to try to kick his way through the shell that seemingly binds him, to destroy the outer forms of limitation that bind his spirit. But there is a step beyond rebellion, a move that is deeper than violent destruction of outer forms of authority and domination. Rebellion when carried too far is always self-defeating. It brings forth new forms of outer authority and dictatorship. It imposes new conformity on its

practitioners and advocates, and on the rest of society if it is strong
enough to enforce its will. Rebellion may bring to light the in-
equities of habitual ways of behavior, but only self-enlightenment
brings freedom.

THE KEY TO FREEDOM

This event from the life story of Jesus gives the key to the freedom all men instinctively seek, whether they live in nature's jungles
or the jungles of modern civilization:

> Turning to the Jews who had believed him, Jesus said, "If you dwell
> within the revelation I have brought, you are indeed my disciples; you
> shall know the truth, and the truth will set you free." They replied,
> "We are Abraham's descendants; we have never been in slavery to any
> man. What do you mean by saying, 'You will become free men'?"
> "In very truth I tell you," said Jesus, "that everyone who commits
> sin is a slave. The slave has no permanent standing in the household,
> but the son belongs to it for ever. If then the Son sets you free, you
> will indeed be free." And "Why do you not understand my language? It
> is because my revelation is beyond your grasp."

CHRIST'S REVELATION

For centuries, the revelation of Jesus Christ has been beyond the
grasp of humanity as a whole. It has been beyond the grasp of
religionist and scientist, of clergy and layman, of educator and
student, of businessman and laborer, of politician and voter, of
rich and poor, of privileged and underprivileged, of black and
white and yellow and any other color. All humanity has been the
slave of the sin of false belief. The "Christian" world has never
really answered Jesus' question: "Why do you keep calling me
'Lord, Lord'—and never do what I tell you?" (Luke 6:46) Only
rarely have enlightened souls penetrated briefly into the revelation
of Jesus, leaving gems of literature such as this one from Robert
Browning:

> Truth is within ourselves, it takes no rise
> From outward things, whate'er you may believe.
> There is an inmost center in us all,
> Where truth abides in fulness:
> . . . and, to know,

Rather consists in opening out a way
Whence the imprisoned splendor may escape
Than in effecting entry for a light
Supposed to be without.

PARACELSUS

The revelation of Jesus Christ is that man is the light of the world, the kingdom or nature of God is within the individual, that each one is the son or descendant of the Most High, and that the authority that is to govern the unfoldment of man in this age is resident within you and me as the spirit of truth. Everyone who disbelieves this revelation commits sin and is slave to that sin—but the light reveals that this slavery is only temporary because the "son" state is the permanent fact of man's being and when the individual enters that realization of his true identity he "will indeed be free." He will begin to experience the new birth, or at least the conception and pregnancy that precede the coming forth of a new creature amidst the wreckage of the old one.

FROM WHENCE COMES FREEDOM OF HUMANITY?

The freedom of humanity cannot come through institutions and organizations; it must come through the awakening and unfoldment of each individual. Institutions and organizations can encourage and inspire the individual growth through their activities, or as has happened so often in the past, they can stifle and suppress it. In the long look of eternity even the darkness, bigotry and suppression tactics of organized society will prove to have been factors in individual unfoldment because the pressures they have enforced on the Man Spirit are finally forcing it to move toward eventual freedom. In the age of enlightenment, institutions and organizations will become what they are in the divine design, instruments of service through which the unfolding Self of humanity finds greater opportunities of service.

YOU ARE THE ANSWER

At this particular crossroads of human experience, it is up to all individuals who are capable of living in the revelation that man is the light of the world to bring about freedom from outer forms of worship, idolatry and violence in their personal experience. This does not mean that one must stop going to church, working in the outer world, or advocating improvement in earthly conditions—but it does shift the scene of action to a deeper dimension of being than the outer rim of life.

The one who is becoming a light in the world is gradually transferring his reliance on outer authority to the authority of his own divine selfhood and is accepting the revelation of the spirit of truth within him as valid and trustworthy. He is coming to recognize ever more clearly that his enemies are those of his "own household," the images and reels of limitation he has imposed or accepted on his own power to be. He is willing to work enthusiastically on his own inner system of images, attitudes and responses and to give up trying to hammer others into molds of his design. The revelation of Jesus Christ is coming within his grasp—it is within the reach of his faith, his will, his understanding, his imagination, his enthusiasm and his authority and dominion.

THE DAWN OF TRUTH

Man is an unfinished product, a still-growing creature, a god in unfoldment. He lives in a universe, whose elements, including his own ignorance, first challenge his spirit and then yield to it. He has come through ages of bondage, ignorance, superstition, violence and war of all kinds. He has been "a bull in the china shop" of creation, wielding fantastic powers destructively in a dark night of preparation to become what he really is—the self-expression of the Infinite. He has lived in a hell of separation—separation from his source, separation from his fellowman, separation from the good every element of his being cries out to experience.

But the light of truth is dawning rapidly in human consciousness —the light seemingly reserved for the "enlightened" is becoming the common, or "extraordinary" property of all mankind. Unenlightened religion, science, business, education, society, politics are all passing into the wastebasket of discarded relics of human bondage. After ages of living on the husks of materialistic beliefs, man is finally, like the prodigal son, coming to himself.

THE HARDEST JOB OF ALL

Self-acceptance is without a doubt man's toughest assignment in consciousness. His religion, science, society and experience have all been solidly aligned against his acceptance of his true identity as a divine original, a unique, indispensable self-expression of the Creative Spirit. All creation has been marking time while man, its leader in the next great step of unfoldment, has been struggling to find himself and to correctly identify his role in the new world. The beautiful story of the prodigal son accurately portrays man's experience in seeking the light. You may wish to reread it in the Bible, but briefly here are the elements:

A rich man had two sons, the younger who asked for his inheritance and went out into the outer world to waste his substance in riotous living, and the older who stayed home, presumably to help his father. The young man who went out into the world (symbolizing man's belief in and reliance on material elements in the universe) had quite a struggle and finally wound up in the corn patch with the pigs where he finally came to himself and returned to the father.

We might say that the prodigal is man and his frantic search for meaning and truth in the outer world—and please note that it was successful! Man's occupation with the so-called physical elements of the universe produced science, and science has probed deeply enough into the material aspects of existence to find evidence of the spiritual source of all things. We might conclude that through science man has come to a degree of himself (truth) and is beginning to return to his father, God, the light of the world.

But in returning, the prodigal runs into trouble, not from his father, but from big brother who stayed at home. The elder son finds little to cheer about in his younger brother's coming home— the younger man does not meet his specifications. The father points out that the older boy has been with him always and all that the father has belongs to him. The older brother did not waste his substance in riotous and superficial living. He apparently thought that his inheritance was some kind of egg, and that if he sat on it long enough, it would hatch!

It is easy to see in the elder brother man's religious practices. Afraid of the world, smug in its self-righteousness, rigid in its concepts, wrapped up in its rules and regulations, sure of its condemnations, the outer church has all too often sat on the truth (all that the Father has) of man's divinity, staunchly resisting the revelations of truth coming through other channels. Religion and science are brothers and now is the right time for them both to drop their suspicions, prejudices and narrow views so both may work together for the enlightenment and freedom of all humanity. There is enough truth revealed through both man's religious and scientific endeavors to free anyone who is willing and ready to live in the revelations. And that's where you and I come in.

THE NEXT GREAT ADVENTURE

Since this is the age of individual unfoldment, the opportunity and privilege of participating in the next great adventure of human progress are open to us, right where we are, regardless of our present status. We may be black, yellow or white, young or old, rich or poor, educated or uneducated from the human viewpoint. We may be in "the cornpatch with the pigs" or smug in our rug of dogmatic religion—we may be religionist or scientist, or a combination of both—but the finger of time is upon us, and we will either be on the "answer" or "problem" side of the current crisis in human evolution. The life current is at flood stage and we will either move in the growing light to the rock of self-acceptance and realization, or be quaking on the sand of lesser beliefs. We will either be involved in violent resistance to forms of outer authority or we will be moving confidently, willingly, understandingly, imaginatively and enthusiastically toward the light of our own inner authority. We will either continue to run to outer authorities for guidance only to discover that for the most part they are less certain than we, or we will come to our self, get acquainted with our built-in authority and learn to follow its guidance.

Jesus indicated that living in the revelation He brought is a step-by-step process, like a seed planted in the ground growing to maturity. So, we will have to muster what authority we have gained thus far, through ideas and courses of action we have shared, plus other experiences and begin right where we are. The idea in the following words will be a good test of your present expression of the power to be authority in action:

I am the authority that governs the images I hold of myself and others.

RATE YOUR IMAGES

Are you? Take a searching look at some of the images you have been entertaining in your household. How would you rate them? Friend or enemy? Yours or someone else's enforced upon you, or that you have accepted on the basis of another's authority? Are they images of light, or of darkness? Of limitation, or of freedom? If these images are the products of your religious, racial, social, educational or economic background, does the integrity within you agree with them in the light of your present understanding—or are they just there through force of habit?

We often hang on to images of limitation long after we have outgrown them. As a counselor, I have talked with many men and women who said that they ran away from home the first time at the age of forty or fifty years, meaning that parental images still ruled their lives. A minister once told a woman who complained that she had been unhappy all her life because her mother rejected her as a child: "You've certainly carried that unhappy image with you long enough. When do you feel that you will be old enough to let it go?" Startled, the woman was quiet for a few moments, then laughed and said: "Maybe I can let it go right now." And she did, with another burst of laughter as an indication of her new-found freedom.

YOU ARE THE AUTHORITY

In a real sense, you have always been the authority that governs the inner images that fill your mind. Consciously or unconsciously you have decided whose opinion or image you would accept. If some outer form or institution seemed formidable and respectable enough, you may have accepted its images and opinions blindly and thoughtlessly. The pronouncements of some church, educational, social or political "authority" usually carry much power in our selection of images.

A man whom I respect greatly told me that as a child he was brought up with almost a "fear" of authorities such as ministers, lawyers, doctors, teachers and other notables. In his early life, he accepted their opinions without question until he began to notice that although they had more training than he in certain specialized fields, they were often much more fearful and uncertain than he in the really important issues of life. When it came to the questions of death, life, God and the destiny of man, he soon learned that his own experience and understanding were just as valid and often much more enlightened than that of the "authorities" he had ignorantly worshiped and served, to his detriment and theirs. Once he began to accept his own right and authority to choose his images, he felt a new freedom, and also a new appreciation and insight into others.

Each person has been given the right of self-determination, and until he exercises that right in the light of truth, he is not making his full contribution to the ongoing of mankind.

THE PRINCIPLE OF SELFHOOD

One of the biggest obstacles to accepting our selfhood is the myth of "selflessness" that has been promoted so diligently by those who are sure that the best way to serve God is to "get themselves out of the way," to become "impersonal." The motives may sound good for this approach; the goal of unselfishness is laudable, but it must be attained through another path than selflessness . . . getting ourselves out of the way . . . or becoming impersonal. There is no such thing as selflessness anywhere in creation because the whole creative process is dependent on individualization or differentiation—or we might call it the "selfing" activity through which the universal finds expression. Without the principle of selfhood there would be no creation, no expression. Through the process of "selfing" the invisible becomes visible, light becomes form, God becomes man, the Father gives all that he has to and through the Son. Even an atom has or is a self—an individual unit of expression—and it hangs on to its self with a great deal of energy as we discover when we break it into its component elements. It has the individualizing power of the universal concentrated in it. Quite likely, the activity of self is in the wave length of light before it becomes a particle. The Gospel of John speaks of the self principle as the Word: "When all things began, the Word already was. The Word dwelt with God, and what God was, the Word was. The Word, then, was with God at the beginning, and through him all things came to be; no single thing was created without him. All that came to be was alive with his life, and that life was the light of men. The light shines on in the dark, and the darkness has never quenched it." (John 1:1–5)

The Word (self-expression of God) is the creative action of God and in it is the life or light of men. Even the darkness of man's ignorance has never quenched the light of his selfhood because it is of God and can never be destroyed any more than God can be destroyed! The light of selfhood responds to acceptance and reveals its full potential only to the one who has the courage and audacity to believe in it: "But those who received him, to them he gave power to become sons of God, especially to those who believed in his name [nature]." (John 1:12)

DRAW ON TREASURES AVAILABLE

In man, the Word, light or self, becomes self-conscious, as it inevitably must, before its full potential can be realized and expressed. Each man is to draw on the treasures available to and through the self of his being and to give it unique and unduplicated expression (give it personality). Far from "getting himself out of the way" each person is to be *the way* the Word becomes flesh, or to phrase it another way, the light shines in the world. To attempt to become "selfless, to get oneself out of the way, to try to be impersonal," is to oppose the flow of creative action and leads to all kinds of self trouble—self-concern, selfishness, insecurity, fear, condemnation, illness and death are the fruits on the tree of this self-rejection and attempted self-obliteration (suicide).

A little observation will reveal that the one who is constantly preaching "selflessness," "getting himself out of the way," and "impersonality" is deeply self-concerned and self-sensitive. Blocking the flow of creative action in any way triggers a reaction in the elements of the self that produces disaster for anyone undertaking it . . . and not only for him, but for the world as well. As any doctor or keen observer of human personality can tell you, each person inflicts his self troubles on all those around him.

DON'T MISINTERPRET JESUS

Much inner conflict has arisen from a misinterpretation of the instruction of Jesus to all who wanted to follow Him. "If anyone wishes to be a follower of mine, he must leave self behind; he must take up his cross and come with me. Whoever cares for his own safety is lost; but if a man will let himself be lost for my sake, he will find his true self." (Matt. 16:24–25) To "leave self behind," or as other translations say it, "deny himself," is to wipe out the sense of limitation that has kept humanity in bondage, it is to open a way "whence the imprisoned splendor may escape." To take up the "cross and come with me," is to stay on the job until the work of obstacle elimination is finished. As Jesus points out, the one who is self-concerned, fearful for his own safety is sunk, but the one who gives up his sense of limitation will find what he really is.

Another misinterpreted observation of Jesus adds to the confusion—He pointed out that, of himself, the son can do nothing; it is the Father within that does the work. And, of course, this is true— the self is the Word, or instrument, through which work is done. The Universal operates through individual or self-expression, much as electricity operates through a light bulb. If the light bulb had self-consciousness, it might well say: "Of myself, I can do nothing. The electricity flowing through me turns on the light." Or the sun might add: "Of myself I can do nothing. I am an instrument through which the light is concentrated and distributed. The light does the work." Note that Jesus does not say: "Of myself, I am nothing." He understood the relationship of the self (I Am) to the Universal. "I and the Father are one." (John 10:30) Dr. George M. Lamsa's translation has it this way: "I and my Father are of one accord." The self and its Creator are one, a unit of wholeness, a complete entity of self-expression. In a growing understanding of self, the individual expression and the Universal are in tune, they are "of one accord." Both join in singing the universal song of self-potential and self-expression: "I Am."

THE UNIVERSAL SONG

Every atom, every cell, every plant, every animal, every man, every woman, every boy and every girl sing the universal song of selfhood: "I Am," in varying degrees. In the light of truth, however, there are those who see that it is really "the Father within," the Creative Spirit, that does the singing through all the instruments of self-expression!

I once became fascinated by a singing bird. In growing delight, I perceived that it was much more than a few ounces of flesh, blood and feathers. I could feel the currents of harmony and music fill every atom and cell of the tiny creature's body until it literally overflowed with song. Occasionally, the bird would pause in silence after it had emptied itself of lilting notes—only to burst forth again in delighted melody when the song had refilled it. The bird sang the song, and the song sang the bird. They were "of one accord." And I could not say where the bird left off and the song began; they were one—a delightful unit of self-expression. The bird did not do the work, if work it was—the song did! But the bird, too, was made of the harmony and music of the invisible world or it could not have tuned in to the song it was created to express.

Until man accepts his own selfhood, he is out of tune with the creative activity that produced him. He is estranged from his Creator and from his fellowmen. He is constantly singing sour notes rather than the harmony he is designed to express. He is insecure, self-concerned, self-sensitive, fearful, selfish, sick, unenlightened. Only by accepting his selfhood, right where he is in understanding, adding to it, realizing that he is the way the light shines into his world, and being willing to personalize that light, can he move ahead on the pathway of self-unfoldment that leads to unselfishness, the sense of security and peace that makes him a light in the world.

In the whirlwinds of rebellion that are now shaking the entire world of mankind, each one can become a peacemaker, first of all in his own being, by exercising the authority of the Word, the light of the world, the divine self that he is. In the authority, the integrity of his own self, his own way, his own person, guided and energized, encouraged and inspired by the Father of lights, the Creator of all, he can choose the images that free him and his neighbor from the bondage of the unenlightened past. He can begin to "straighten up this shape—touch it again with immortality —give back the upward looking and the light."

ACTION AND THE WORD

An authority in any field is the one who is competent in it, who is active in it. Following are courses of action in a written version of the Word, that you may want to use to exercise your power to be authority in action:

At long last, I accept myself as a permanent and vital part of the creative process of the universe.

I stop trying to obliterate myself, to get myself out of the way, to become impersonal. I joyously accept myself as the way and the personality through which the light shines into my world.

I am old enough, and young enough, right now, to release all the images that have limited my capacity for self-expression.

With a growing sense of authority and conviction, I reject and eject all inferior pictures from my imagination chamber.

I joyously exercise the inner authority that is mine as a self-expression of the Infinite.

I believe in the authority that is mine as the light of the world. I am willing to exercise this authority. I appreciate my growing understanding of the authority that is mine. I authorize only the images that free me and my fellow man to be the light of the world. I am enthusiastic about the wonderful way my whole being responds to the authority of my awakening selfhood.

I accept myself without reservation, so completely that I move step by step from self-concern and selfishness to self-assurance.

I accept my own self-identity so confidently that I no longer doubt my neighbor's.

I gratefully exercise my authority to stimulate the flow of radiant energy into self-expression through me.

I learn to use my authority on and in myself—not on my neighbor.

I exercise my authority to accept my unity with my Creator. I and my Father are of one accord. I am in tune with the harmony of the universe.

I authorize the light of the world to lift the performance level of all my systems of self-expression.

I am grateful for the authority that transforms me from the inside out.

SELF-ACCEPTANCE

The revelation of Jesus Christ leads to self-acceptance. To live in this revelation is to know the truth that sets you free from the mental bondage of the past, the false images shaped by ignorance and superstition. This is to be "born again," to be baptized by the Holy Spirit, to be washed in the blood, to be crucified and to be resurrected from the tomb of self-ignorance and to enter the activity of self-enlightenment. You are now preparing to be a self-governing unit in the world of tomorrow, a living experience that will call forth the authority and dominion inherent in all men. You may appreciate the following words:

I am no longer elated or deflated by the opinions and actions of others. I am learning to be true to the integrity and authority of my own soul.

Until we have accepted and are developing our "self," we have nothing to give up, to share with our world, to be unselfish with. The selfhood of man, or if you prefer, the selfhood of God, is the building block of the world of light and freedom. All human progress, and also all divine progress, has come through a great self, a great person who was willing to become the way a great revelation of truth was made available to humanity. Take a personal look down the dimly lit corridors of history and see for yourself. Your self is not expendable—it is expandable. It is not to be destroyed—it is to be unfolded and shared with your world!

THE POWER TO BE:
LOVE

As you exercise your authority to establish new images in your imagination chamber, you will discover, like the rest of us, that the false, unenlightened images of the past have deep roots—they have feelings attached to them. The violent, distorted pictures of the Creator, himself and his fellowmen that man has supported and implemented have been emotionally grounded—they are anchored in man's feeling nature, and the final freeing action of the light of the world takes place in man's emotions. It is not enough to know the truth mentally, we must also come to know it emotionally—to feel it. Man knows intellectually (at least, much of humanity knows) that there is one God, the Father of all, and that humanity is one family, but his actions do not yet carry out his knowledge because his feelings stand in the way. Man is still largely governed by his feelings of separation, fear, suspicion, resentment and greed. The light has dawned in his mind, but it still has to penetrate his heart, out of which are "all the issues" or actions of life. Man must not only "know" better to "do" better—he must also "feel" better.

THE ROOTS OF LIGHT

Fortunately, the light of the world also has roots. It radiates from, and is anchored in, the nature of the Creator, the feeling of love. The spirit of truth that Jesus said would lead us into all truth is not only the revelation of truth, it is also the feeling of truth—or the feeling of love. The feeling of love is the spirit of truth that ultimately leads us into all the good that has been prepared for expression through us! All great religions unite in proclaiming that love is the energy that fulfills the law, that completes our own divine nature. Modern researchers into the nature of man join the same chorus of love.

Man must not only educate his mind through the revelation of truth, he must let his heart be educated by the feeling of love. The feeling of love "casts out fear," dissolves all feeling of separation and returns man to the feeling of unity with his Creator. "God is love," and the feeling of love is unity with God. Unity with God leads to unity with all of His creatures. The feeling of love is the unifying influence that links all creation into one great symphony of life. The feeling of love is the light of the world at work in our emotional nature, and as it deepens and expands through exercise our whole being and life are transformed. The purpose of the remaining chapters of this book is to help stir the feeling of love into a mighty, healing, renewing current of energy in you and me. To the best of my ability, I am writing these words with a feeling of love, and it delights me to feel that you are reading them in the same spirit.

TO FEEL LOVE

Now that we are beginning to realize that words are an expression of the Creative Word, we can appreciate and increase their effectiveness in opening our being to the light of the world that we are. Every written statement is the image of a course of action, a verbal treasure map that we can profitably follow. Consider the course of action in the following statement until you get the "feel" of it:

> The light of the world that I am flows into my emotional nature and stirs up the feeling of love in me.

Now give your attention to the feeling of love, and something pretty wonderful will begin to take place in you. To feel love is to feel God, and to feel God is to "practice the presence" of God, to share in the activity of God. The resulting ecstasy might be described as "delicious." What really happens is that the vibration level of the fields of living energy in which you live and move and have your being is lifted by the inflow of light and love, and even the cells of your body and the relationships of your outer world respond.

You are experiencing a degree of what religious terminology might describe as the "outpouring of the Holy Spirit." The light of the world is intensifying its action in and through you. You are leaving that limited habitat of the prodigal, the cornpatch and the pigs, and returning unto the Father, who has a great feast ready to celebrate your return to the land of the living. Do not try to prolong this feeling of love and ecstasy. Let its healing, renewing, resurrecting currents flow through you, but do not try to hang on to it, or it may literally burn you out. Our mental, emotional and physical systems of self-expression are not unfolded sufficiently yet to handle the current for any great lengths of time. This flow of energy is what Emerson describes as "the current that knows its way." You can trust it and know that in its flow through you old images of limitation, and the patterns of thought and feeling they have produced, are being erased.

You need not despair and search frantically for this feeling if it seems to disappear—it has merely passed from the level of your conscious mind to penetrate into the subconscious depths of your being where it continues its freeing activity. It will surface again— you will become conscious of it again, and your understanding of it will continue to grow through experience. Remember, the light travels in waves but always in an ascending spiral—and you can know that the light of the world and the feeling of love are with you forever. They are permanent elements of your being, and they will never leave or forsake you.

GOD IS LOVE

The biblical statement "God is Love" is perfectly accurate. God is not a superman dishing out love to you and expecting it in return. God is love, and you are its instrument of self-expression. To love God is to experience the feeling of love—to let love flow through you. As you let the feeling of love unfold and grow naturally, you will come to understand and participate in its activity. You will soon be experiencing the action described in the following words: "The feeling of love draws me closer and closer to God, and I begin to feel that I and the Father are one," and "The feeling of love casts out fear, wipes out all sense of separation, and unifies me with my Creator."

THE APPROVAL OF LOVE

God is love and in that love there is no condemnation, disapproval, or faultfinding. Love always welcomes its children back into the fold. Love always approves of its creation, regardless of the stage of unfoldment it is in. No matter how many eons, universes, incarnations and civilizations humanity is away from its destiny, love approves of it because it is only in an atmosphere of approval that creative action works constructively. In an atmosphere of disapproval, creative action becomes destructive as it is in the world today. Love (God) approves of you as its child or self-expression. It approves of you as the light of the world, the image of God. It approves of you as a human being, its vehicle of expression. It approves of you as a man or woman, boy or girl. It approves of you whether you are a doctor, lawyer, minister, businessman, worker, prostitute, thief or in any other human role because it is only in the atmosphere of approval that you are open to receive the light, the radiant energy of love, that frees you from bondage. The approval of love never varies, unlike the sliding scale of human values.

Interestingly enough, the images of self-righteousness at the top of the scale of human achievement are often more difficult for love to dissolve than are the painful images at the bottom. It is pretty hard to accept help of any kind if one is wrapped smugly in the robes of respectability, complacency and know-it-allness, while the painful images in the seemingly lower echelons of humanity often cry out for help. "Lord, be merciful to me, a sinner," it hurts!

In any event, of this you may be sure: whenever love catches up with you, it always puts the stamp of approval on you so that you will feel free to open up and receive the radiant energy that

improves you! Love is unconcerned about what is wrong with you—
it knows what is right with you!

Words like the following can help you to accept the approval of
love:

The feeling of love reveals the approval of my Creator.

God approves of me as its child, image and self-expression.

*God approves of me as a human being, as a man or a woman, boy or
girl.*

God approves of me and my efforts at living thus far.

*In this atmosphere of approval, I accept the light, inspiration and feeling
of love that wipe out false and limiting images and the fear they have
produced.*

I am secure in the approval of Divine Love.

THE UNFORGIVABLE SIN

It is amazing in this supposedly enlightened age how many
people feel sure that God has dropped them from the approved list.
Someone has convinced them that they have committed the "unforgivable sin," and they are doomed for eternity. Some of the
"unforgivable" sins that men and women have carried around for a
lifetime would be almost laughable if they were not taken so
seriously by the burden bearer. It is a relief to learn that the
"unforgivable" sin is a sin against the Holy Spirit. It is always a
closed state of mind and heart that refuses to permit the Holy Spirit
or feeling of love to do its work of healing, renewal and forgiveness.

This unforgivable state may be brought about by a variety of
causes, including a feeling of separation from God or humanity,
complacency, a prolonged feeling of guilt and condemnation, indifference, or just plain pigheadedness. This unforgivable sin or
state can be brought to an end instantly by the one caught in it
any time he is willing to accept the feeling of love that returns him
to the Father's house and the approval that lifts him from bondage.

I have rejoiced many times to see the burdens of a lifetime
drop off the shoulders and out of the minds and hearts of persons
who realized for the first time that only their own fears and
condemnations stood between them and freedom. Jesus pointed

out that the love of the Father is like the light of the sun—it shines on the just and the unjust, but the unjust are blind to its rays. Or like the rain that falls on the enlightened and the unenlightened, but the unenlightened resist or are unaware of its refreshing drops.

LOVE IMPROVES

Let the feeling of love return you to the approval of your Creator where the radiant light of being cleans your inner slate and sets you off on a new path of improved living. Love never leaves you where it finds you—even as it approves of you, it improves you.

If you want biblical confirmation of the approving activity of love, read the story of creation again with feeling. You will find it in the first two chapters of Genesis in the Old Testament. You will find that the Creator put the stamp of approval on each mighty stage of the creative process (saw that everything was good), including the stage that produced that much-maligned creature, man. Only man gets fed up with man, thereby stopping or suppressing his own progress. Love always approves of its self-expression even when he is going through trying experiences. Disapproval always cripples, suppresses and distorts the spirit of man. In the atmosphere of approval, love at work, even the hardened criminal, confirmed bigot or bored intellectual is helped to find himself.

LOVE AND EVIL

Does love then approve of evil? No more than light approves of darkness, or health approves of illness, or life approves of death. Love is creative action, and it always clears the deck for improved and increased activity, an activity that must be expressed through each person. Love, the Father of lights, says in effect: "Son, I am glad you're back home. You've done a lot of living and have picked up some 'unforgivable' sins such as fear, a feeling of separation, condemnation, self-righteousness and narrow-mindedness . . . so let's clear the decks. I approve of you for you are my son, and I know your potential. In this atmosphere, the feeling of love, let all that stands between us go, and as we celebrate your homecoming, the barriers you have erected between us will be swept away. You will soon be ready for a fresh start, and this time, remember that I am with you always, with you as the feeling of love that reminds you of my presence." Your inner voice may speak in a slightly different language, but you will get the point as you let the feeling of love expand in you. Your world will get a new message, too, as you let the feeling of love accelerate the flow of light into self-expression through you. Let your light shine so that men attracted by its radiance will recognize its source, the feeling of love, active in you and available to them.

LET LOVE ENTER

Before you practice the Drill in the Light the next time, let love put the stamp of approval on what you are doing. Let the feeling of love add a new and deeper dimension to the experience. Put your faith into the feeling of love, be willing to surrender to it, rejoice in your growing understanding of it, let it capture your imagination, be enthusiastic about it, and let the feeling of love govern your exercise of authority. You are moving into a whole new phase of self-unfoldment. You are beginning to experience the greatest power in the universe—love, the creative energy that brought you into being as its self-expression. As you exercise your power to be love in action, you will not only know the truth that sets you free, you will feel it.

14

THE POWER TO BE:
WISDOM

The wise man always uses the greatest energy available to him in
meeting the problem or opportunity presented to him for fulfillment. The wise man also knows that the greatest problem or
opportunity he will ever find is his own growing, unfolding selfhood and his relationship with other people. Here, in the words of
our Bible, we find how the great teacher, Jesus Christ, put the
combination to some of the wise men of his day: "Hearing that he
had silenced the Sadducees, the Pharisees met together; and one
of their number tested him with this question: 'Master, which is
the greatest commandment in the Law?' He answered, 'Love the
Lord your God with all your heart, with all your soul, with all your
mind.' That is the greatest commandment. It comes first. The
second is like it: 'Love your neighbor as yourself.' Everything in
the Law and the prophets hangs on these two commandments."
(Matthew 22:34–40) These two commandments were not original
with Jesus. They appear in the Old Testament and in other forms
in great scriptures of the world. Jesus, however, singled them out
as the greatest and wisest instruction and went so far as to say
that on them hang the law and prophecies of all time, which can
well mean that all revelations of truth are "hung up," or blocked,
until these two commandments are carried out.

A DEEPER LOOK

Love brings its own wisdom and good judgment, and since the two commandments of love are the distillation of the wisdom of the ages and the present, a deeper look at the course of action involved is in order. These "love" commandments are traditionally interpreted to mean that we are to love God first, our neighbor and then ourselves, quite often in that order. Any approach to loving God, neighbor and ourselves produces remarkable results— but suppose we take an even deeper look. The following words from I John 4:16–18 (Phillips translation) give deep insight: "So have we come to know and trust the love God has for us. God is love, and the man whose life is lived in love does, in fact, live in God, and God does, in fact, live in him. So our love for Him grows more and more, filling us with complete confidence for the day when he shall judge all men—for we realize that our life in this world is actually his life lived in us. Love contains no fear. . . . Indeed, fully developed love expels every particle of fear, for fear always contains some of the torture of feeling guilty. This means that the man who lives in fear has not yet had his love perfected."

PASSPORT TO PARADISE

First of all, this wonderful insight gives us incentive for carrying out the commandments to love and to become wise in its ways. As love is developed in us, it expels every particle of fear, inner torture and guilt. Every doctor of the mind in the world would turn handsprings of sheer joy if he could expel fear, guilt and the torture they produce from his patients. He knows, as we all do if we look into the matter, that fear and its retinue of guilt, condemnation, inertia, indifference, suspicion, and all the other "devils" that prey on humanity are the real obstacles to health, peace, and effective living. What a potion to prescribe as an antidote and solvent for the cause of all illness—LOVE, the highly specialized energy that casts out fear. The more we love (express God), the less we fear—and when love is perfected in us, all fear is gone. Love promises a passport to paradise.

THE FIRST COMMANDMENT

Now for a look at the first great commandment of love: "Love the Lord your God." Note the object of love: "The Lord your God." That makes it pretty specific, does it not? Not the Lord, the Catholic, Lutheran, Presbyterian, or Metaphysical God—but *your* God. And your God could be nothing more and nothing less than your present consciousness (awareness, understanding, working knowledge) of God. Since God is Love, the Lord your God is your consciousness of Love, or your feeling of Love. Again, a reminder: "God is love, and the man whose life is lived in love does, in fact, live in God, and God does, in fact, live in him." We love that feeling of love, the image of God, the Divine Presence, the Christ, the kingdom (nature) of God, when we let it grow (be perfected) in us, and we do this through total commitment or surrender to it, when we agree to becoming its instrument of self-expression, "with all our heart, with all our soul, with all our mind."

The light of the world, which is working in us, reveals that its source is love, much as a ray from the sun would lead us to its source if we accepted and followed it. Love, the nature of God, is in reality the pearl of great price, and the light of the world is its radiation. We surrender to love when we give our attention to it, and exercise our power to be in it. We live in it. We have been dwelling in the revelation of light, and now we are ready for an even deeper experience in living. We commit ourselves to the feeling of love (the Lord our God), we surrender to it, we value it, cherish it, worship it—it becomes more real and substantial to us as we put our faith into it, become willing to let it express through us, grow in our understanding or working knowledge of it, picture ourselves as its image and likeness, are enthusiastic about it, and authorize it to govern our whole being—heart, soul and mind, with our body, home, finances and all other activities thrown in for good measure.

SOME VERBAL TREASURE MAPS

You will find it easy and adventurous to follow the following verbal treasure maps or courses of action:

I believe in the feeling of love in me (the Lord my God) with my whole being, and it becomes real, substantial and active in me.

I am willing to let the feeling of love deepen, expand and express through me.

I rejoice in my growing understanding of the feeling of love.

I gladly picture myself as the expression of love.

I am enthusiastic about the feeling of love as it stirs into powerful action in me.

I authorize the feeling of love to govern my emotional, spiritual and mental nature (heart, soul and mind).

I commit myself completely to the love that is God. I am interested in it, I praise it, I appreciate it. I am governed by it.

THE LOSS OF FEAR

Without any doubt at all, you are engaged in the most important activity of your entire life. You are dealing with and experiencing the nature of God, and you are being prepared for a whole new life. You are plugged into your source, and as your feeling of love grows, fear is expelled and you are more confident of your role in the day of judgment, which is every day. You know and feel that love is your judge—and you no longer fear judgment because love's judgment is always healing, forgiveness, freedom, growth and unfoldment. To those who say, "Yes, God is a God of love, but He is also a God of justice," you can reply either silently or audibly: "I know, and I no longer fear His judgments because I am beginning to understand and feel what love is." The realization may come to you quietly as it did to me one early morning in the California desert near Palm Springs:

> This morning our Father called me early
>   To watch Him woo His world awake.
> In growing wonder, I watched God gently take
>   The veil of slumber from each living space,
> And saw that not a single universe—or mountaintop—
>   Or blade of grass—or floating cloud—or singing bird—
> Was out of place.
> All creation had been forgiven, cleansed, refreshed,
>   Made new by the divine embrace of night.
> In the dawning light,

The exultant sun poured its golden benediction from above—
And suddenly I felt—and understood
That God is Love.

(PUBLISHED IN DAILY WORD MAGAZINE)

YOUR DIVINE HOMECOMING

You will know and feel a peace that comes only through unity with God, your divine homecoming. As St. Augustine beautifully phrases the matter: "O God, you have made us for yourself, and our souls are restless until they rest in Thee." It is only the feeling of love that brings the peace that "passes" or brings understanding. The feeling of God in the heart surpasses any intellectual knowledge. ". . . While knowledge may make a man look big, it is only love that can make him grow to his full stature. For whatever a man may know, he still has a lot to learn; but if he loves God, he is opening his whole life to the Spirit of God," our delightful companion in the adventure of living, St. Paul, puts it.

THE WISDOM OF LOVE

In the wisdom of love, you will see that the judgment that brings punishment, suffering, fear and death is the judgment passed by man himself—the judgment of separation from his Creator and the judgment of refusal to let the feeling of love govern his attitudes first of all toward himself and then toward his neighbor. You may feel this more, at least initially, than you understand it or than you are able to put it into words for transmission to others. But the feeling will grow and unfold in wonderful ways until you come to realize that to "love the Lord your God," to let the feeling of love take over in you and govern your being is really to love yourself. As you let love expand its presence and power in you, you become its self-expression, and you are love in action.

To love God is to love yourself because you and God are one in love. This is the secret of the first great commandment, and that is no doubt why Jesus said: "That is the greatest commandment. It comes first." This commandment comes first, not so much in order of importance as in order of execution. The second commandment is like it. There is no way to love your neighbor unless love is active in and through you!

THE GROWTH OF WISDOM

As the feeling of love grows in you, your wisdom grows, too—and soon you will be able to do what love does. (The son does what He sees His father doing!) You will be able to approve of love's immediate instrument of expression—yourself. You will be able to bypass judgment based on appearances and go to the heart or truth of your nature (practice righteous judgment). You will put the stamp of approval on yourself boldly, even audaciously, because your sense of separation and fear is being expelled by the feeling of love, the action of God redeeming you. You are now wise enough to know that unless you are willing to step out of the atmosphere of disapproval into the environment of approval, love cannot continue its miracle of transformation. We might say that approval is the opening shot that brings the full power of love to bear in our unfoldment and growth. In the parlance of the prize ring, approval is the left jab that sets our opponent of fear up for the final punch of victory.

In the growing confidence that the feeling of love is giving you, you are probably ready to stand up on your spiritual feet and declare:

I do what I see Infinite love doing—I put the stamp of approval on myself as its instrument of expression.

I approve of myself as the image of God—the light of the world—the self-expression of love.

I approve of myself as the feeling of love at work.

I approve of myself as a human being—a growing, unfolding, confident, enthusiastic representative of love on earth.

I approve of myself as a man (woman, boy or girl).

I approve of myself where and as I am in the assurance that love is already moving me out of any state of limitation.

I stand firm in my self-approval, regardless of appearances, and I give thanks for the improvement that love works in me.

STAMP YOURSELF WITH APPROVAL

If you are like most of us, you may find it is quite an experience to put the stamp of approval on yourself. We have lived under the blanket of self-disapproval for so long, it seems natural. At least, it has become habitual through centuries of practice. Often I have asked persons to go home, stand in front of their mirrors, and repeat statements of approval to themselves. Some have said that at first, they just could not do it. Others, including women and professed "strong" men, have told me that they burst into tears and sobbed. Some discovered, to their amazement, that they had lived a whole lifetime without really approving of themselves in any way.

Small wonder that so much of humanity is fearful, sick and burdened by guilt and condemnation. We have been taught by experts (including our own ignorance) to disapprove of the handiwork of God, our own radiant self. We have crucified the Christ again and again because we have judged by the appearance of present conditions and performance, and thus we have effectively blocked our personal improvement and unfoldment. Love is not concerned with past mistakes—it is the God "of the living"—it always approves of our present potential as its instrument of self-expression, and we can enter confidently and joyously through the door of improvement—self-approval.

YOUR BODY AND YOU

Once you get the "feel" of it, putting the stamp of approval on yourself as the self-expression of Infinite love becomes easier, more joyous and more effective. You will be surprised at how many areas of your being have been laboring under the burden of disapproval. Take your body, for example. A fine minister once told me that he was surprised that some people could remain in their body at all—they disapproved of it and its functions so thoroughly and often. Put the stamp of approval on that wonderful residence now. Following are verbal courses of action:

I approve of my body as the temple of the living God I am.

I approve of my hands as the working tools of love.

I put the stamp of approval on the organs and functions of my body as the instruments of Infinite love.

I approve of my breathing as the breath of the Almighty.

You will find many simple and happy ways of freeing yourself so that love can work its miracle of improvement in and through you. An executive of a large company told me that he started in as a salesman and had such an inferiority complex that he dreaded to call on his customers. He used to drive around the block hoping that he could not find a parking place so he could get out of making a personal contact with a "tough" customer. Then somewhere he picked up the idea that he should begin to love himself and while on his way to make calls he would sing, and even sometimes shout: "I love me. I approve of myself as a salesman." His sales began to pick up, and he started to enjoy selling. In fact, he became so successful that his boss gave him a desk job and he was not too sure he wanted to give up selling, so he still made calls just to keep his hand in.

Love isn't formal or stuffy. It is a gay and romantic energy and delights in those who approach its treasure stores audaciously, lightheartedly, joyously expectant of a happy reception by the Father of lights, the giver of every good and perfect gift. It is not even religious—Use your own words and approach, after all, you are only carrying out the commandment: "Love the Lord your God with all your heart, with all your soul, with all your mind."

THE SECOND COMMANDMENT

As the feeling of love perfects itself in you, you will find that the second commandment: "Love your neighbor as yourself," is not nearly as burdensome an assignment as you may have been led to believe. It is really a natural unfoldment of the first commandment, and the feeling of love is too great to be hoarded. It must spill out into your world—it must be shared because once you have had things straightened out with your Father, your love reservoirs will naturally overflow.

I am not being facetious, nor playing down the importance of what we are doing—but I am reminded of what Jesus, that ardent promoter of the love commandments, said: "Be of good cheer. I have overcome the world [the world of disapproval and suspicion, fear and doubt]." Perhaps that's the commandment we most often break: "Be of good cheer." You might want to approach the second commandment in this frame of mind and heart: "I cheerfully approach the action of loving my neighbor as myself." I know you will have your times of trial, but at least that puts you off to a good start.

You are to love your neighbor as yourself, and that means in the same way and the same courses of action.

NO MINOR SKIRMISH

As a start, we might put the first action in these words:

I do what I see Infinite love doing—I put the stamp of approval on my neighbor as its self-expression.

Then we can get to more specific cases and focus the range of our loving action. We will find that love is no minor skirmish—it will not be satisfied until we have worked out new relationships with everyone in our lives, including those specialized neighbors we may have labeled enemies. But start with the "easy" ones— those you already have much affection for, such as a member of the family or close friendship circle. As a suggestion, do your work silently, even a close friend or relative might consider you a likely candidate for the psychiatrist's couch if you just barge in and start speaking. Love and approval are effectively transmitted without many words anyway—they form an aura or atmosphere that envelops all in your world. Words can, and they will, come later.

TO START THE FLOW OF APPROVAL

Here are words, written and silent, to start the flow of approval:

I approve of you as the image of God—the light of the world—the self-expression of love.

I approve of the feeling of love at work in you.

I approve of you as a human being. A growing, unfolding, confident, enthusiastic representative of love on earth.

I approve of you as a man (woman, boy or girl).

I approve of you where and as you are in the assurance that love is already moving you out of any state of limitation.

I stand firm in my approval of you, regardless of appearances, and I give thanks for the improvement that love works in us both.

DON'T WITHHOLD APPROVAL

It is perhaps easier to approve of another as the image of God—or the light of the world—than as a human being. For most of us, these are abstractions and not as disturbing as the human element of expression is so often. But in the wisdom of love, you will see that to withhold approval from someone because his "humanness" does not satisfy you is in the same category as refusing to shine a light into a room because it is too dark. To withhold approval and short-circuit the flow of love into another's life is to deprive him of an opportunity to be healed, freed, inspired, returned into the fold of love. The way he responds or fails to respond to your approval and love is, of course, his business—but in making them available to him, you are following the second commandment.

There is so much disapproval of the human element in the world that I want to take this opportunity to put in a plug for the human being. After all, if love did not desire or need human beings as instruments of self-expression, it could have brought forth something else. As far as I know, the human being is easily the most remarkable creature in the universe, at least on the earth where I have to live for the time being. To be human is to be able to work as co-creator with the Creative Spirit, God—it is to be able to feel and express love—to think—to believe—to image—to dream and to bring forth—to unhook the atom—to harness the cosmic energies of the universe—to be a devil or a god in the making—to dream of and no doubt to achieve immortality.

Where does humanity begin and divinity end? Can you tell me? I hereby put a stamp of approval on humanity, even its present chaotic state, as the self-expression of God, the growing, awakening, magnificent family of the Creator. As with others, perhaps with you, too, human relations has been quite an experience for me, but there have been wonderful times when love has flashed at least a bit of light into my contacts with the human family, and I felt that:

I love people—
  all kinds of people.
The tall ones, the short ones,
  The round ones, the square ones,
    The pretty ones, the not-so-pretty ones,
      The brown ones, the black ones,
        The white ones, the yellow ones,
          The any-color ones,
            The ones I understand and
              The ones I am yet to understand.
I love people—
  I have watched them meet prosperity, adversity,
    triumph, defeat, joy, sorrow, life and death.
  I have worked with them, prayed with them, played
    with them, agreed with them, argued with them, and
I love people—
  I think they are wonderful.
  God must, too. He has made, and keeps
    right on making, so many of them.

(FROM DAILY WORD)

I think I am not fooling myself—this is more of a "treasure map" than a road I have traveled in actual practice, but the thought has made me willing to try to put the stamp of approval on a much wider range of human beings than I would have dreamed possible in earlier stages of my jaunt through the "human" scene. Jesus pointed out that it is relatively simple to love and approve of those who agree with us and slap us on the back in appreciation, but that real growth comes through loving our "enemies"—those whose appearance, actions or disposition arouse negative reactions in us. Those who need love and approval the most are usually the hardest ones for us to "handle" but they are also undoubtedly the ones we most need to learn to love and approve for our own personal growth. In any event, the wisdom of love urges us to keep right on releasing love to the best of our growing ability in all relationships.

LOVE THROUGH APPROVAL

A young boy came home from his first week in school and announced that he just didn't like one of his teachers. She was many things she should not be, according to him, and he felt that he just could not stand her for another day. After a conference with his mother, he agreed to start blessing this teacher several times a day—"blessing" is certainly a form of love and approval—and guess who was his favorite teacher by the end of the school term. Yes, you are right!

Love acting through approval works miracles at any age. I once visited a clinic operated by an outstanding physician who is incorporating music, painting, and what I would call "love" therapy into his medical practice. I was privileged to have a long conversation with one of the women who was finding healing through this unusual treatment, and I asked her if she could tell me what she felt was the most important factor in her improvement. She thought for a long while before she answered: "I feel it was the fact that the doctor and all members of his staff approved of me, no matter what I did or what I told them of my past. They accepted me and loved me as I was, without criticism or disapproval. I couldn't believe that they were sincere at first, but after a few weeks I began to improve. After considerable time I went home for a brief stay, and I could hardly wait to come back to the clinic. I guess I wasn't convinced even then—I wanted to see how they would treat me on my return. I had the same approving, loving reception, and I feel that I am finally coming out of the woods." She told me that she had felt rejection and disapproval all her life and for the first time in her experience met a group of people who approved of her as she was. This was more important to her than medicine or other forms of therapy.

Human relations is the most urgent area of human endeavor. Once we solve "human relationships" in love, our other problems will be well on their way to solution. Racial, religious, social disapproval, blocks the flow of love that is the only energy capable of establishing peace and understanding on the earth. International disapproval and war are the sum total of individual attitudes; so put the stamp of approval on yourself and your neighbor and let the feeling of love flow out to bring light into the world. The wisdom and good judgment of love are operating through you.

15

THE POWER TO BE:
JOY

As love expands its operation in our lives we are lifted more and more into the harmony of the universe and a new order is developed in our experience. We are plugged into the source of all good, the light and love of our inner being, and we are no longer so dependent on other people or certain set patterns in the outer world for our happiness. This does not mean that we do not appreciate others or the outer world; in fact, we will appreciate them more because we no longer have to expend quite so much energy trying to enforce our tight little patterns of order—what we think is right or wrong—on them. We no longer have to pass judgment quite so often or violently on the appearances and disappearances in the outer scene. Our sense of order becomes less rigid; it acquires a flexibility that enables us to flow with life, rather than fight our way through a world that seems intent on going its own way, particularly when we try to hold it in a certain pattern of behavior or stability.

DON'T TRY TO CARRY THE WORLD

After a lecture in New York City one evening, a shining-faced young man came up to me and blurted out: "You really mean that all I have to do is to love people? I don't have to worry about them, or correct them, or get upset by them? Wow, what am I gonna do with all my spare time?" He did not give me a chance to suggest that in his spare time he could begin to see the people who had caused him so much concern in a new light. He could accept and approve of them as they are, and begin to appreciate them, perhaps for the first time. He could begin to enjoy people and things, rather than be concerned that they fit into a particular pattern of his choosing.

We all know mothers and other housekeepers who are so determined to have their outer surroundings in apple-pie order that they keep members of their families or guests in misery by insisting that everything be in its right place at all times. There are bookkeepers who turn a whole company upside down in search of a misplaced penny. There are reformers who are in constant misery because so much of the world flouts their sense of moral order. There are those whose whole world is upset by the introduction of a new idea or course of action. We have all, I am sure, had considerable experience in trying to get some part of the world or someone established in what we know are "right" ways, according to our standards of order and perfection—only to discover that our concepts are either rejected or did not fit the situation or person involved.

From personal observation, I have just about concluded that this old world doesn't sag even a quarter of an inch when I stop trying to carry it. Naturally, we all have responsibilities in the outer world of which we are such a vital part, and we need to meet them as efficiently as possible—but what a relief it is to begin to transfer much of that responsibility to a power that is greater than anything we have yet experienced. There is an outer sense of the rightness of things, which often takes the pattern of rigidity and unyielding insistence that everyone and everything conform to it. This conformity stems from the judgment that there are only certain ways to do things and that other ways are wrong. Our judgments usually tell more about us than they do our environment, and when we insist on certain narrow patterns, usually for others, we are probably saying that we are fearful—afraid that we will be unable to cope with anything we are not accustomed to, or afraid to trust the power of love in another.

JOY IN ORDER

As you grow in love, you will detect a subtle change in your attitude toward others and outer things. I cannot dictate an order for you to follow, but I can almost guarantee that you will soon develop an inner sense of rightness, a feeling of order that can best be described as joy.

Jesus left this message for all who are willing to let love govern their lives: "If you keep my commandments, you will abide in my love, just as I have kept my Father's commandments and abide in his love. These things I have spoken to you, that my joy may be in you, and that your joy may be full." (John 15:10–11) This joy is the product of the activity of love. No doubt as love expels fear from our minds and hearts we are returned to our true order, the state of harmony or unity with our source that is Joy. This joy is not a feeling that we force to exist, it comes quietly and deeply on its own terms—and these are that we live in love.

We may suddenly realize that some time has elapsed without our being worried or concerned about ourselves or others. Or we find that some outer evidence of disorder no longer upsets us as it would have at an earlier stage of our lives. Even temporary setbacks in our plans no longer have such a disturbing influence in our thoughts and emotions. It is easier for us to laugh at ourselves and with others, and living becomes a much happier experience than ever before. Surprisingly, a new sense of order is apparent in outer affairs, too. Our health usually improves, our business prospers, and our relations with others develop new meaning and depth. We have much to do; in fact, we may be busier than ever before, but the old sense of burden is lifting and we are enjoying whatever we are doing.

The following words may well describe an activity which you detect taking place in you:

My feeling of love is establishing a deep joy in me.

Joy and enthusiasm are closely related, and you may be developing the following attitude:

I meet life's assignments with joy and enthusiasm, with a growing confidence in the power of love to handle them all.

RELEASE FROM WORRY

You will no doubt be able to release any anxious hold on others in the joy of knowing that the resources of love are available to them, that your faith in love active in them is of great benefit, and that if you are to take outer action, love will let you know when and how. You will be delighted at how often the affairs in another's life are righted so soon after you stop interfering in them. Obviously, the wisdom of love will guide you to look out for those whose age or condition necessitates it, but you may be surprised at the change in your concepts of dependency.

As joy deepens in you, you will flow more easily with the harmony of the universe; you will be in tune with the "music of the spheres." Praise and appreciate the joy that love gives; it is a permanent part of your make-up.

ENJOY WHAT YOU HAVE

Joy, like our other spiritual muscles, grows—once it is established—through exercise, both conscious and unconscious. Perhaps our most effective, and certainly one of our most pleasant, forms of prayer, is simply to enjoy what we already have. As you exercise joy consciously whenever the opportunity presents itself, you encourage its subconscious development, and often you will feel joy bubbling up from its inexhaustible source, love within, and you may find yourself chuckling or laughing quietly just for the "fun" of it. This is not usually the "Minniehaha" type of enjoyment, but a quiet, inner rising up of your whole spirit from the bonds of unhappy thought and feeling.

Your experience may fit words like these:

I enjoy being alive. It's great to be alive, and I am finally discovering it.

I enjoy thinking constructively and optimistically.

I enjoy what I am doing.

I enjoy living completely in the present moment and event.

I enjoy my work, my family, my friends, my home, my co-workers.

I enjoy my growing ability to relax and let life live me.

I enjoy letting go of some of the burdens I have insisted on carrying.

I enjoy loving the Lord my God. I enjoy loving my neighbor as myself.

SHARE YOUR JOY

Joy, enthusiasm, praise, and thanksgiving are all from the same wonderful family of effective prayer. To enjoy anything is to appreciate it—to increase its value in your life. You will discover that joy is a gift that you give and that you receive. It comes from the activity of love within, and you give it to your world which gladly responds in its own way. There is nothing more inspiring than to watch someone who enjoys living, enjoys his work, whatever it is, enjoys people.

Before each practice of the Drill in the Light, and before each element of it, remind yourself: "I enjoy and appreciate what I am doing." Do the same before embarking on any other course of action we have shared in this book. Practice enjoying (putting joy into) your exercise, your breathing, your thinking, your feeling, your sleeping, your eating—into every area and activity that concerns you and you may join in the sentiments expressed by a friend of mine: "After years of trying to carry the world on my shoulders, of mentally and emotionally auditing the lives of people around me, I am finally learning to relax and let go. I never knew life could be so enjoyable."

16

THE POWER TO BE:
STRENGTH

Joy and strength may seem to be strange partners, but the Bible assures us that "the joy of the Lord (Love) is your strength." Light, love and joy operating through us, give us a vigor and vitality, the strength of resiliency and flexibility—an ability to roll with the punches of life and to maintain our balance in the face of criticism and challenge, both from outer sources and our own often unruly states of mind and heart. A happy, joyous personality is the strong one. An unhappy, unappreciative person is always near the exploding point, and it often takes little outer pressure, or inner turmoil, to unbutton him mentally and emotionally. He is always coming apart at the seams. Joy, the natural harmony and order of the universe of love, is our strength.

OUR INNER FIELD

Our conviction of the reality of the light and love of our inner kingdom is becoming strong enough so we find it not quite so necessary to defend it, or to inflict it on others. We will probably discover that our former attempts to convince others of the truth of our inner revelation was for the purpose of convincing ourselves.

As a woman told me once: "I am finally sure enough of the reality of this inner light that I no longer yield to the temptation to hit other people over the head with it. It is shining strongly in me, and when the light is strong enough, it will come to the surface. After all, the sun does not argue with people, it just shines!"

This new sense of selfhood, our own inner integrity, which perhaps began as a flash of lightning in the dark sky of our world of limitation is gaining the strength and vigor to stand on its own feet. The mustard seed of faith, planted in the field of light is beginning to assert its own right to exist. There may still be plenty of "weeds" in our inner field, but the new plant of light and love is beginning to make room for itself. As Jesus put it: "The kingdom of God is as if a man should scatter seed upon the ground, and should sleep and rise night and day, and the seed should sprout and grow, he knows not how. The earth produces of itself, first the blade, then the ear, then the full grain in the ear. But when the grain is ripe, at once he puts in the sickle, because the harvest is come."

Once the seed is planted in the field of light, we go about the business of living—eating, sleeping, working—and the plant draws nourishment and strength from the radiant earth in which it is growing. Naturally, as good "tillers" or gardeners we take care of the plant, through exercise, prayer and meditation, especially during its formative stages—but we soon become aware that a new reality is being established in us. Eventually "the harvest is come" and we put in the sickle and begin to reap some of the benefits. We do not suddenly reach a high plateau and stay there forever. This is a growing, eternally unfolding harvest, and an inner strength and vigor are part of it. One "harvest" is but the seed of another planting, and our growing strength enables us to keep on growing.

THE GROWTH OF LIFE

I once gave a lesson on "School Is Never Out," pointing out that life is a constant state of growth, that perfection is not a static heaven, but a healthy, vigorous activity that never stops. I was surprised at the reaction of a number of the listeners who apparently felt that if they could only muster enough strength to make it into heaven, the need for growth was over. We need to find the strength, the vigor to grow eternally (at least for the foreseeable future), to accept change and opportunity to express more light, love and joy.

Prognosticators of our earthly future tell us that in an "ordinary" lifetime, many people will find it necessary to change professions or lines of work two, three or even four times because of the mushrooming discoveries of modern science. Every once in a while, we read a medical pronouncement that it may soon be possible to live in the same body for as long as 150 to 200 years! Spiritual prophets have long predicted immortality, an eternity of growth and unfoldment, and the vigor and desire to live forever will come from the joy of the Lord, our own inner selfhood. The promise is that the government will be completely on "His" shoulders, and while we are all a long way from joining Jesus (and no doubt many others) on the throne of mastery, we are at least beginning to govern the tribes of Israel—which is an involved way of saying that we are getting strong enough to discipline the powers of our own Spirit!

Rejoice in the growing strength of your own inner selfhood. Stand tall in the stronghold of your own integrity. More and more you will be able to stand in peace, the strength of soul that moves you from being a "fighting" element to being a "lighting" element in the world.

17

THE POWER TO BE:
FORGIVENESS

In our unfoldment in the light and love of our inner being, we reach a point where we are strong enough to practice renunciation or forgiveness at both the conscious and unconscious levels. To renounce is to let go of the bondage of the past, to forgive ourselves and others, to unburden ourselves, to deny the power of past experience to limit us in our present living. Forgiveness is stressed over and over again in the Bible as well as in all great teachings as absolutely essential to our individual growth and well-being. Unforgiveness, of ourselves and others, is the "unforgivable" sin that blocks the activity of the Holy Spirit (the spirit of oneness, wholeness, light, love and joy) in us. When we are unforgiving, we are at best in a state of stagnation or non-growth; we are prisoners of our own past, a clogged channel in the stream of life. Unforgiveness—disapproval, guilt, condemnation, damnation, hell, fear, resentment, hatred, dislike—is always hardest on the one who practices it. Forgiveness is always self-forgiveness. In any event, it starts with the self of us. When we forgive another for his "sins" against us, we deal first with our own reactions to and judgments of his action or lack of action.

WHAT IS FORGIVENESS?

Quite often, the "sins" of others exist only, certainly most vividly, in our own consciousness—others may be blissfully unaware of how they have "wronged" us. When we are unduly self-concerned and sensitive, almost any act can become a "sin" in our sight. The hurts and resentments that are buried in most of humanity are as much the product of the individuals carrying the load as anyone else's responsibility. As the feeling of love expands in us, fear and resentment are decreased, and forgiveness becomes more spontaneous.

To forgive goes beyond "forgetting" or "excusing" ourselves or others for past or even present actions. It literally means "to give" ourselves a new and improved reaction to what has happened or is happening. It is doubtful that we ever really "forget" or "excuse" anything—we merely bury it in our memory, and it remains unforgiven unless it is brought to light by some process of healing so we have another chance to improve our reaction and judgment. Forgiveness and growth are twins—they go hand in hand. We need forgiveness not only for "bad" reactions, but for lukewarm, bored, indifferent ones also. To be completely integrated into the vivid, vigorous, healthy stream of growth that is life, we go beyond halfway measures.

UNCHAIN THE PAST

Our memory, being the storehouse or consciousness of soul, is perfect. We can never forget anything that has happened in our long and often "checkered" experience of living. Some events seem to be forgotten, but that merely means that they have been buried for one reason or another beyond conscious "recall" by conventional means. Not only are the events themselves assimilated into our memory system, so are our reactions to them. Our reactions, or judgments, become part of our images and attitudes—and are thus projected into our present living pattern.

It is wonderful to know, though, that while we cannot forget our past, we can change it! The events themselves cannot be changed, but the most important aspect of the past, because it is alive in the present, can be changed in the light of our present understanding or consciousness. Guilt, fear, resentment, condemnation, disapproval—the tortures of hell—can be erased. Brighter reactions than these—the past reactions of joy, appreciation, love, understanding, can be deepened and expanded. The past, our past, is always subject to change. It is subject to our growing power to be forgiveness in action. If you are a member of the large group that holds to the traditional belief that faith in Jesus' sacrifice is the only way to forgiveness, fine. But each one will still have to accept and implement that forgiveness.

I am sure you will be interested in this account of the healing power of forgiveness as recorded in Matthew 9:1–8:

> And now some men brought him a paralytic lying on a bed. Seeing their faith Jesus said to the man, "Take heart, my son; your sins are forgiven." At this some of the lawyers said to themselves, "This is blasphemous talk." Jesus read their thoughts, and said, "Why do you harbor these evil thoughts? Is it easier to say, Your sins are forgiven, or to say, Stand up and walk? But to convince you that the Son of Man has the right on earth to forgive sins"—he now addressed the paralytic—"stand up, take your bed, and go home." Thereupon the man got up, and went off home. The people were filled with awe at the sight, and praised God for *granting such authority to men.*

THE HEALING POWER

I was told the story of a woman who was suffering from an incurable (unforgivable?) disease. She went to a "faith" healing meeting and was told to mentally put all her sins out on a chair in front of her so that when it was her turn (she was in a large meeting) for the minister to speak the healing word, she would be forgiven. She was puzzled because she thought she had forgiven herself and all others for all the wrongs she knew anything about, but since she was desperate, she followed instructions. When her turn came, she reported that she felt a tremendous flow of energy throughout her whole being, then a great relief and release, and she went home forgiven and healed.

Most of us are paralyzed to some extent by our need for forgiveness. We might say that some element of unforgiveness has short-circuited the electric and electronic circuits of our body, distorted the living fields of energy in which we exist, and blocked the flow of light and love into self-expression through us. Even if our "paralysis" consists only of inertia, complacency, confusion and indecision, we need to exercise our growing power to be forgiveness or renunciation in action.

Charles Fillmore, co-founder of the Unity movement, said that we should practice forgiveness consciously at least once a day. He suggested that we sit down at the end of the day's activity, before retiring, and mentally forgive ourselves and others for all sins of omission and commission. We should never go to sleep in an unforgiving and unforgiven state of mind. Those who feel that "I just can't forgive so-and-so," or "I just can't forgive myself," will benefit from this conscious practice of forgiveness, and eventually the forgiving action will take place. After all, man did not fly on his first attempt, but he is in the process now.

THE ART OF FORGIVENESS

Here are some verbal guidelines for practicing the art of forgiveness consciously:

I joyously issue a blanket decree of forgiveness for myself and all others in my life.

I am glad that I have grown strong enough to be forgiving, of myself and others.

The feeling of love in me forgives the negative reactions of my past.

The light of the world I am, wipes out the limited reactions to the events of my past, and I rise into a new sense of freedom.

I review past events in the light of my present consciousness, and I easily and joyously improve my reactions to them.

In the name and through the power of Jesus Christ, I forgive myself and others.

HOW MUCH TO FORGIVE?

You know your capacity for forgiveness better than I do—so use the words that release its healing action in you. Even brief attempts at forgiveness will bring beneficial results. I feel from personal experience and the shared experiences of others that just the realization that we can forgive and be forgiven is one of life's greatest boosts toward ultimate freedom.

We should be in sad straits indeed if we were dependent only on our conscious efforts to practice forgiveness, essential as they are to our growth. Love itself is constantly on the job of forgiving us, of freeing us from the bitter or binding judgments of our past living. We may never become conscious of all the forgiveness love works in the silent reaches of our being, but in many ways we can co-operate with its freeing action. Love is "of too pure eye to behold evil"—it never hangs on to anything unlike or opposed to its own wholesome nature, and it is constantly bringing events to our conscious attention so that we can do something constructive about our past reactions to them.

NEVER FEAR THE PAST

Now that we understand this process, we need not fear "remembering" unpleasant experiences. They are not brought to our attention by some "devilish" power to torture or plague. It is love on the job, saying something like this: "Skipper, I think you have grown to the point where you can release your old negative reactions to this event. I have been on the job in your insides, and if you but say the word, we can heal this experience once and for all—or at least we can improve it enough so we can file it again as a blessing instead of a curse. The next time I bring it to your attention, if that is necessary, you can do an even better job of forgiving." At this juncture it is your opportunity to say to the event and the people involved in it: "I forgive you. Thank God, I forgive you and me, too." Be alert to these constant opportunities, and you will experience miracles of freedom from past "sins."

RELIVING YOUR LIFE

Many who have been close to death and returned to full consciousness report that one of their last memories was an apparent review of all the events of a lifetime. This was the action of love, giving them an opportunity to pass an improved verdict before moving ahead on life's next assignment. I had an experience, similar to this, on a prolonged trip to Africa several years ago.

I was a long way from being dead, but I had been under constant strain in unaccustomed surroundings, short water supply, unusual food, and a rigorous schedule of three or four lectures a day, plus traveling from village to village over what my delightful companions called roads but which I labeled "affirmations"; to this was added the stimulation of new friends and experiences—so I was in an unusual state of consciousness.

One night, I was sleeping on a cot under a mosquito netting. I had fallen asleep instantly when my head hit the pillow. I don't know what time it was when I returned to conscious awareness, but I was sitting up laughing involuntarily and uncontrollably. My friends, who were sleeping at some distance, must have thought that a new brand of laughing hyena was on the prowl. Suddenly I stopped, also involuntarily, and became quieter than I have ever been before or since; an inner door opened in my mind and I saw my whole life—not just one lifetime—in clear detail. I could see and feel people, events, experiences; I suppose that in an instant I relived the whole history of my soul from its inception to that moment.

A NEW FREEDOM

In that flash of recall, I saw that everything was good—that even the people and events that triggered painful judgments and reactions were part of an over-all plan of unfoldment on that endless pathway of life. Suddenly again, I felt a wave of gratitude flood over me, and I stood erect and free for a brief space in the presence of love, forgiven and forgiving, understood and understanding, approved and approving, loved and loving. Unafraid I breathed the fresh air of heaven. Before the shrouds of ignorance claimed my mind again, I could see that I was in truth a son of light—beloved, forgiven, healed, and complete—and so were all those sons and daughters of light who had worked with and "on" me in the past. I quickly returned in consciousness again to my surroundings, and I was a sleepy, tired and somewhat puzzled "human" on a cot in the African bush. I have never recaptured the feeling and the freedom of that moment of release again, but they have never completely left me either. I find that I am not quite so quick as I used to be to pass judgment on myself and others . . . I don't want to have to "undo" any more unhappy verdicts than is absolutely necessary.

Forgiveness and renunciation are both denial and affirmation. Practiced consciously or involuntarily through the growing feeling of love in us, they deny the power of past mistakes in judgment and reaction to bind us in the present, and they affirm the power of love to establish new attitudes in the present for experience in the future. Life is a continuity, and it is good to know that eventually we all have the past, present and future in our growing consciousness of light, love and life itself. Before your next drill in the light, accept your growing power to be forgiveness in action, and you are on your way to a new freedom in living.

18

TIIE POWER TO BE:
LIFE

If the words attributed to Jesus are accurate, He must have affirmed life with a boldness and power that startled His listeners. Even today His words have power to electrify the dullest mind, lift the heaviest heart. He was on a life mission: "I came that they may have life," He said, "and have it abundantly." The kingdom of God is within man, and he is the light of the world was His inspiring proclamation. There is little evidence to indicate that the abundant life He proclaimed began after death; in fact, He said: "Whoever lives and believes in me shall never die."

YOU AND YOUR GROWTH

In the courses of action outlined in this book, you must have had at least an occasional drink out of the "spring of water welling up to eternal life." At the minimum, if you have really stirred up the light of the world that you are and exercised your powers to be, you are more radiant and energetic, more ready to be confident, willing, understanding, imaginative, enthusiastic, decisive, loving, wise, joyous, strong, forgiving and lively! You are much better acquainted with the kingdom of God within. You may hesitate to say that you are "born again" of the Spirit, as

Jesus advocated, but at least you are moving in that direction because you are more "spirited"—the light of the world and your powers to be are all qualities of Spirit, as you can readily see. You are no longer so firmly attached to person, place or thing, even though you are learning to appreciate them all much more deeply than you did when you were "possessed" by them. You are learning to flow with life, to stir up your inner powers, and to love your neighbor as yourself.

EXTERNAL DIVIDENDS

While these are all spiritual developments, they bring immediate dividends in this so-called material world, too. Anyone looking for a delightful companion, effective employee, or inspiring employer would certainly give happy consideration to these qualities of the spirit. Even a flower, or an animal, would enjoy the pleasure of your company. As these qualities in you are developed further, you will naturally be in line for promotion in any type of endeavor, your salary might even be increased without begging on your part—and you would see the wisdom of seeking first the kingdom and its right use because the things you need would be "added," not by magic but by the miracle of growth and unfoldment of your own divine potential capacity for living! You are discovering the connection between heaven and earth and have no doubt stopped trying to separate the Spirit from the rest of you.

A CREED FOR LIFE

Life is the light of the world that you are, according to the Bible. To gain an added depth in exercising your inner powers, you may wish to try the following courses of action:

I believe in life.

I am willing to surrender to life.

I give thanks for a working knowledge of life.

I get a new picture of myself as the image of life.

I am enthusiastic about life.

I authorize life to work its miracles through me.

I love life, and life loves me.

I am wise in the ways of love and life.

I enjoy life.

I am strong in life.

I forgive myself for all the restrictions I have placed on life.

I live life and life lives me.

I am the eternal life of God, the light of the world.

TO INHERIT THE KINGDOM

You either are now or will be soon ready to make the transition in consciousness that St. Paul describes in the following words:

> Thus it is written, "The first man Adam became a living being"; the last Adam became a life-giving spirit. But it is not the spiritual which is first but the physical, and then the spiritual. The first man was from the earth, a man of dust; the second man is from heaven. As was the man of dust, so are those who are of the dust; and as is the man of heaven, so are those who are of heaven. Just as we have borne the image of the man of dust, we shall also bear the image of the man of heaven. I tell you this, brethren: Flesh and blood cannot inherit the kingdom of God, nor does the perishable inherit the imperishable. (I Cor. 15:45–50)

There is only one way to inherit the "kingdom" prepared for us and that is to get rid of the false belief that we are just flesh and blood. We have been carrying around the dusty images of the old man Adam long enough. He was just a living being—he existed, but he had little notion of where he came from, where he was going, or why he was here on the earth. He did not really care—he fed his face and stomach, caught his wife or wives, brought forth children and installed his dusty image in them through the process of religion or education or experience . . . and so the whole human family became men of dust.

WE ARE MORE THAN FLESH AND BLOOD

But the dust got so thick that some men began to question the validity of this type of blind existence; they probably became quiet and listened for something beyond the chatter of the man of dust, and a light began to dawn. In that dawning light there are many radiant names—Moses, Isaiah, Buddha, Mohammed, Jesus Christ, Paul, John—plus, I am sure a whole host of the unnamed who perceived that man is much more than a man of dust, destined for a dusty end, or a fiery end, or even a gold-plated heavenly end. They saw that man is in reality the image of God, the light of the world, a life-giving Spirit in his own right, and they tried to bring the good news to dusty old Adam man. Naturally, they were tortured, maimed, crucified—that was dusty's way of handling those "nuts" who saw what he couldn't see, felt what he couldn't feel, understood what he couldn't understand. And, you might ask, what were the leaders of the ruling establishments of religion, education and society doing? For the most part, they, like the Pharisees and Scribes of every age, were real busy jotting the "jots," tittling the "tittles," and padding the dogmas that Jesus said kept them from entering the kingdom and blocked the entrance for others.

THE DAWN OF A NEW AGE

But there is no profit in condemning the past. We are all part of it, and it of us. A new age is dawning, and the Spirit is being poured out on all flesh. Pharisees and Scribes along with the rest of humanity are receiving an injection of radiant energy—and the truth is breaking out all around the world. We are finding through science that even the dust is radiant energy in concentrated form, and that man is a life-giving Spirit, self-expression of the universal creative energy, being prepared for his role as joint governor of the world of tomorrow.

Those who are ready for the inner transition will gladly trade the "image of the man of dust" for the "image of the man of heaven"—the light of the world, a life-giving Spirit. They won't suddenly disappear from the earth—they may be "dropouts" from the world of false images—they will be running our businesses, working in stores, driving busses or flying jet planes, doing all kinds of service jobs and probing more deeply into the nature of the universe in scientific laboratories; they will pop up in our religious, educational and social institutions; in our nightclubs, radio and television stations, publishing plants—Oh, they will be all over the globe. You may suddenly find one in your own family—it may be you!

YOU AND YOUR NEIGHBOR

The inner transition will follow a decision that resembles closely the course of action in the following words:

I have had enough of the man of dust image. I accept my real identity as a life-giving Spirit.

Get the feel of what you are reading and saying. Words of this type stretch your spiritual muscles.

Then extend the same recognition to your neighbor with a feeling of love and appreciation:

I have had enough of carrying a "man of the dust" image of you. I accept your real identity as a life-giving Spirit.

As you start carrying this true image of your neighbor, you will see him in a new light. You will begin to get the feel of the wonder that is man. You will understand why you cannot put anyone into a pigeonhole. Man is not a pigeon, not even a man of the dust. He cannot be bottled up in tight little compartments. He does not fit into a Catholic, Protestant or Metaphysical bottle. He does not fit into a biological, chemical or flesh-and-blood bottle. He does not fit into a black or a white or an "any color" bottle. He does not fit into a social, moral, business or labor bottle. Not even the "man of dust" really fits into any bottle—His spirit is always breaking through in some way. You will have a deepening respect and admiration for the individuality of each person. You will get flashes of insight into the meaning of the Fatherhood of God and the Brotherhood of man.

Eventually the "man of the dust" image will be unimaginable to us and some of the practices that we have associated with this image will be gone, too. One day it will be as unimaginable to drop bombs on our neighbors as it is now unimaginable for most men to practice cannibalism or sacrificing human beings to nonexistent gods. We will no longer be able to "see" ourselves doing the barbaric acts that are habitual to the "man of the dust." Life will be richer and more meaningful. You will be vitally interested in all men for you will recognize each one as the infinite, magnificent self-expression of the One Creative Spirit, appearing as many.

ESTABLISHING THE SPIRIT IMAGE

It will take time and discipline to get the life-giving Spirit image established. We have carried the false one for a long time, and old man Adam will poke his dusty head into our imagination chamber for some while before he disintegrates. But at least we will know that he is on the way out. Work joyously to keep your new image on the throne of government. Here are some exercises in words:

I am a life-giving Spirit expressing myself in the light of the world.

I am a life-giving Spirit expressing myself through a miracle-working faith, a dynamic will of good, a growing understanding, a vivid imagination, a vibrant enthusiasm, a deepening inner sense of authority and decision.

I am a life-giving Spirit expressing myself through a feeling of love, wise action, a sparkling joy, a resilient strength, a forgiving attitude, a thrilling sense of aliveness.

I am a life-giving Spirit expressing myself through a healthy mental, emotional and physical body.

I am a life-giving Spirit expressing myself through a prosperous business, a helpful profession, or any activity of which I am a part.

I am a life-giving Spirit expressing my infinite potential through inspired thinking, healthy emotions and constructive action.

THE LIMITLESS POTENTIAL

The areas of potential exercise are numberless. The earth is our realm of expression and it is no more limited than the infinite powers to be that lie in the heavenly realms of our own being. As a life-giving Spirit man will soon be roaming freely in both heaven and earth. After all, he is the power to bring forth a new heaven and earth at the impulse of the creative power that brought him into being.

How far do we go? Paul states that this Spirit is given us by God as a guarantee that life will swallow up our mortal elements and we will become immortal. Jesus says that to follow the courses of action, to live in the revelation He brought will lead us to eternal life. These predictions no longer seem so farfetched. Science already points out that in a very real sense the so-called physical universe is immortal—it goes on forever, a constant flow of living energy. Even the smallest particle does not disappear without a trace—its form may go, but it only goes back to its component parts. Forms, organisms, nations, civilizations and universes come and go—the living energy that sustains and forms them and the new replacements is indestructible. Researchers even speculate that our much-underrated body has elements of immortality—it has the capacity of renewing itself, unless interfered with.

ETERNAL LIFE

Eternal life has much more than duration—it is not merely the prolongation of man-of-the-dust existence, human longevity. It is really the end of that sense of existence and the beginning of another higher-quality experience. As you get the feel of your real identity, a life-giving Spirit, you will join many others in the opening stages of eternal life. You will come to know and feel that you as a life-giving Spirit, the image of God, outlast all the mental, emotional, physical, social, and other forms through which you find ever-greater expression. Fear of death will gradually recede, if it has not disappeared already, and your emphasis will be on life. A beautiful friend of mine, somewhere in her eighties, or should I say, eternities, told me that everyone should be working on at least one "impossible" project to keep life interesting. By impossible, I am sure she means beyond the reach of our present understanding. So eternal life seems like a likely project for co-operative experimentation. We will have plenty of company. Scientists around the world are getting into the eternal life act, and although they may not speak our language at all times, their discoveries will continue to be a source of inspiration. The following course of action in words can get us started:

I am a life-giving Spirit, and the life I give is the only life there is, the eternal life of God.

THE TWO OF US

Hold this image of the man of heaven for yourself, for me and for your neighbor of every race, color and creed. I will do the same for you. We would not be flying now if the life-giving Spirit had not whispered into some open mind and heart: "You can fly. Go ahead, try it." If all who were nudged by the flying impulse had responded: "I can't. It's impossible," man would still be earthbound, not even dreaming of exploring the unfathomable depths of outer space. I have reached the point in this incredible age where I will believe anything that is "good." Eternal life has a delightful ring to it, and I am willing to probe the depths of inner space, beginning right now. Let me know if you discover something that you feel will give me a boost.

Thank you for reading this book. Its message, as I pointed out elsewhere, is you. For whatever it is worth to you, I put the stamp of approval on you as the light of the world, a life-giving Spirit. I approve of you as a human being. I approve of you as a man, woman, boy or girl. May your life experience be rich, fulfilling and adventurous as we walk the eternal pathway of light and love together. It's great to be alive and to be part of the Creator's greatest product, humanity!